Funny Old World

R P Jones

Alastair Ross

J Harry Smith

Howard Hague

Previous Inquirer Columnists

FUNNY OLD WORLD

Sideways observations
from The INQUIRER

JOHN MIDGLEY

LENSDEN PUBLISHING

Lensden Publishing
© John Midgley
Published 2016

ISBN: 978-0-9575891-3-1

Printed by MTP Media, Beezon Fields, Kendal, Cumbria, LA9 6BL

Contents

FOR CELIA, WITH LOVE AND
FOR ALL WRITERS FOR AND READERS
OF THE INQUIRER WITH GRATITUDE.

Preface and acknowledgments

The *Inquirer*, founded in 1842, enjoys its claim to be the oldest established and continuously running nonconformist newspaper in Britain. In its early days it was one of a number of such papers in the Unitarian movement. Despite the decline in organized religion and the trials and tribulations of the ensuing years, it is the one that has survived. Along the way, one other has appeared on the scene, *The Unitarian*, a monthly owned by the Manchester District Association of Unitarian and Free Christian Churches.

The *Inquirer* has tried to serve our denomination in a number of ways. It is not simply the organ of the General Assembly of Unitarian and Free Christian Churches. It is owned by an independent company and has always been managed by its own volunteer board of directors. This has given it an independence and freedom which it has cherished, enabling it to comment on and sometimes challenge denominational governance and activities. More broadly it has been a forum for the sharing of ideas and opinions, as well as news of various activities and involvements. In the era of online publications and electronic social media, *The Inquirer* finds it something of a struggle to remain a positive presence in print, but remains determined to do so.

This present volume is intended to put into more permanent form a collection of observations on events in the world and among our congregations and various dimensions of the movement. It is all written from a personal standpoint, in the hope of stimulating interest and prompting the reader's own reflections. It is hoped that readers who are not Unitarians might also find the comments of interest, as giving an insight into one Unitarian's take on the ways of the world in the early years of the 21st century. We are a small denomination that often feels overlooked and neglected, but we regard ourselves as a welcoming community, happy to share our ideas, opinions and enthusiasms with all.

Particular thanks are due to my friend and colleague Leonard Smith, for enormous, invaluable, practical help and encouragement in the production of this book. I am grateful always to my wife Celia, an avid reader and frequent contributor to the *Inquirer*, my chief critic, in the best sense, careful proofreader as well as being constant in support and encouragement. My son Nick has also helped with proofreading and encouragement.

Thanks are also due to the several ministers, editors, colleagues and friends who, over many years, have encouraged me to put my thoughts into writing, as I have tried to do likewise to others.

A number of abbreviations and acronyms are used in this book:

GA is the common abbreviation for our denomination, the General Assembly of Unitarian and Free Christian Churches.
B & FUA means the British and Foreign Unitarian Association, our previous governing body which now exists for trust management purposes.
UUA is the Unitarian Universalist Association of America.
ICUU is the International Council of Unitarians and Universalists.
MCO (later HMCO) is the Harris Manchester College, Oxford.
UCM is Unitarian College, Manchester.
UU means Unitarian Universalist.
IARF is the International Association for Religious Freedom.

Introduction

The diary or notebook column is a familiar feature of newspapers and journals. The title suggests that the writer has recorded some events or jotted down some observations, and is now sharing them. The column is usually the product of one writer, though in the *Guardian* it is shared among several. The comments are usually on current social, political or religious matters, from an individual point of view. Almost anything goes for subject matter, though I have always tried to answer positively the question, 'Might these readers be interested in this particular matter, now?'

The Inquirer, for which I have produced Funny Old World for more than four years, has had columns of this sort for many decades. The earliest was probably that produced, originally anonymously, by a Unitarian layman, Ronald P Jones, beginning in the 1920s. He had a particular purpose in mind. At that time, the two organisational bodies of the Unitarian movement, the British and Foreign Unitarian Association and the National Conference, were considering an amalgamation. This was a difficult, even contentious matter. RP Jones's purpose was to share some of the thinking and debates at the meetings of these organisations. He wrote about it up and until the time the two bodies amalgamated into the General Assembly of Unitarian and Free Christian Churches in 1928. His observations, then, are something of an historical record.

RP Jones chose to write in the style of Samuel Pepys's diary, even taking the great diarist's name and heading his columns, 'Mr. Pepys at the

Conference'. During the second world war he took up the *Inquirer* editor's suggestion of reviving the column, this time writing on his general wartime experiences, under the title, It is Very Observable, one of Samuel Pepys's favourite phrases.

Some years later, beginning in 1958, Alastair Ross, a member of Golders Green Unitarians, began writing under the heading, Layman's Notes and later, Reporter and Thinking Aloud. For thirty years this was one of the most popular features of the *Inquirer*. Along the way, other writers had created notebook columns. In the 60s and 70s, Rev. J Harry Smith (1893-1981) wrote his Northern Notes and It Occurs to Me. Another layman, Howard Hague, shared his Thoughts While Riding By in the 1980s. Again, these were personal observations on matters of concern and interest to *Inquirer* readers and others.

Alastair Ross's death in 1992, only a couple of years after his contributions had ended, left a gap. Commencing in the Spring of 2011, I decided to try to fill it.

Typically, in a diary or notebook column, a number of topics are covered and the paragraphs are usually short. This can easily give the impression that the matters in hand are lightweight, but a column of this sort is no hodgepodge. A few glimpses into the writer's personal life are allowed, but mostly serious topics and troubling ideas are reflected upon. These frequently prompt reader responses.

A further feature is the frequent use of humour. RP Jones's Pepysian style was a device to enable him to be critical in a light-hearted way, for example in his memorable dig at over-long sermons: 'Lord, how these parsons do mistime their discourses!' Thus he offended no-one. Alastair Ross often raised a thoughtful smile and J Harry Smith was known for his wry northern humour, both of them clearly aware that not far below the surface, serious points were being made.

Unforgettably, J Harry advised me, as a young minister, 'Don't be afraid of using the same sermon more than once. After all, a carpenter doesn't buy a new saw every time he wants to saw a block of wood.'

That he wrote under the title, It Occurs To Me, prompted me to find a phrase to use as a title. I chose Funny Old World as I had learned, as a youth, to distinguish whether something funny, written or spoken, was either 'funny-peculiar' or 'funny-ha-ha'. I like the idea of Thoughts

While Riding By, though Howard Hague was never on a high horse or hobbyhorse. Nor did any of these writers pursue grudges, and apart from RP Jones they sidestepped denominational politics.

From these previous writers I have learned a great deal. They were always a reassuring presence in the *Inquirer*, exploring topics that interested them. Reading them was like engaging in a friendly conversation, or receiving a welcome letter from an acquaintance. Nor can I imagine that either the present *Inquirer* editor, or any of her predecessors, would permit the diary to degenerate into what has been described as its scurrilous second cousin, the gossip column, however much some readers might enjoy that!

2011

Of ministers, first cousins and a trip to Massachusetts

2011

Of ministers, first cousins and a trip to Massachusetts

Humanist bopper, Insha'Allah mayor

This first sharing of thoughts and observations appeared just after the annual meetings of the General Assembly of Unitarian and Free Christian Churches. I was reflecting on those meetings, including the unique experience of our banner parade being 'danced in' by a group of women, catching up on news of other events in the world, paying a visit to my local Quaker meeting house and trying unsuccessfully to remove some graffiti.

Good to see Sir Peter Soulsby on the platform at the General Assembly Meetings in Swansea with the Executive Committee, though no longer as its Convenor – and in fact he no longer serves on the EC. No mention was made of his recent relinquishing of his seat in the House of Commons and his post as Opposition Spokesperson for the Environment. We are very coy about party politics. Sir Peter had escaped for a while from campaigning to become the first-ever elected mayor of Leicester. An encounter in the dining hall gave me a chance to ask, "Why quit the national for the local in politics?"

"It gives me a chance of a real job, one where I feel I can make a difference," he replied.

I pondered whether to ask if the opposition spokesperson post is
'unreal', but stayed with the elected mayor campaign.

"Will you win?" I asked.

"As my Muslim friends in Leicester say, *Insha'Allah* (God willing)," he
grinned, then added, "And the bookmakers have me at five-to-one on
to win; and they've stopped taking bets."

Sure enough he gained a thumping majority, which means he is to
Leicester as Boris Johnson is to London. There the resemblance ends.
"There will still be a Lord Mayor of Leicester," he assured me, "for the
more ceremonial occasions, a bit like our GA President. And that's
good."

Alas, this means we no longer have a Unitarian in Parliament. And
that's not so good.

*

Sad to learn of the recent demise of Donald Dunkley. He has had little presence on the Unitarian scene for many years, but one small claim
to fame is that he was (probably) our last ministerial conscientious
objector. As a convinced pacifist he refused the call-up to national service in the mid-1950s. He was also an enthusiastic and campaigning
humanist, in the days of the so-called humanist versus theist controversy. I recall him carefully selecting hymns from *Hymns of Worship* that did
not have the word 'God' in them. Nowadays we are more likely to speak
of having religious humanists among us, to distinguish them from anti-
religious voices from the British Humanist Association and elsewhere.
It's a helpful distinction.

Donald once told me that for light relief from the stresses of training
for the ministry at Unitarian College, he would take himself to the local
Levenshulme Palais for the Saturday night hop. There he cut quite a
dazzle on the dance floor. His ministry at Buxton with Great Hucklow
was brief, before he departed into social work. Perhaps our ministry

didn't have room, then, for a pacifist, humanist bopper. Does it now, I wonder? Go on, surprise me!

*

Email bulletin from Hope Not Hate, a campaign group established in 2004 to counter fascism and racism, tells me that its prime target, the British National Party, suffered hundreds of losses in the recent local council elections. There are certainly no BNP councillors to be found in Peter Soulsby's Leicester, and none in my home town of Skipton, though I was surprised to see some graffiti scrawled on a wall near the local station. Beneath the BNP initials, someone had added 'racist thugs'.

I'm inclined to think such a response only attracts more attention to the publicity. Can anyone recommend an effective graffiti remover?

*

A sad anniversary of sorts was in my mind at our Annual Meetings in Swansea. Some folk remembered our last visit to that city in 1965, but I seem to be the only person who recalled that those meetings were buzzing with the news of the murder by racists, only a few weeks earlier, of 38 year-old Unitarian Universalist minister James Reeb. He was in Selma, Alabama, having been on a civil rights march. We joined hands and sang 'We Shall Overcome' in his memory. The world reeled in shock at this tragedy and Martin Luther King preached a passionate eulogy called 'Who Killed James Reeb?' at his memorial service. This was not simply a rhetorical question. The FBI's Cold Case Initiative is reopening the investigation into the 46-year-old case.

*

Our Assembly having agreed unanimously to affirm our support for the Charter for Compassion, many ministers and Lay Preachers will be leading worship on the theme in coming weeks. To assist with this, former librarian and retired minister Andrew Hill, ever the maker of lists, has "done a rapid word search through our three hymn books...of the numbers of the hymns which actually use the word 'compassion'. There are no doubt other hymns about compassion but which don't actually use the word itself." I'm sure he would be happy to share his findings, but something in me thinks it would be healthier for us all to do our own research. My own musings on this lead me to remember that 'compassion' is linguistically the same word as 'sympathy', a word somewhat out of favour, 'empathy' being preferred. There is a difference, which is worth researching too.

*

PS to the Annual Meetings. It seems to me that there were fewer attenders at this year's gathering. At a morning meeting for worship at our local Quaker Meeting house, which I've been to a couple of times, the clerk to the meeting stood up at the end and said, "Anyone thinking of attending our Yearly Meeting (their equivalent to our Annual Meetings) in July in Canterbury had better book soon as accommodation is running out. Over 800 people have already booked." It would be interesting to learn what our spiritual first cousins do at their yearly meeting. Bet they don't have a banner parade, certainly not one led in by dancing women.

May 2011

Keeping an eye on our first cousins

I enjoy keeping a weather eye on groups that we feel closest to on the religious scene, wondering how Quakers, Liberal and Reform Jews are getting along. To a fair extent I also regard the Guardian *as a sort of ally, not least because of its historical origins and its track record on social justice causes. And I am not averse to friendly contacts with more orthodox Christians, when they will have us.*

I usually refer to the Quakers as our spiritual first cousins. A sort of first cousin once removed, from the Christian to the Jewish tradition, might be the Liberal Jews, presently celebrating the centenary of their 'flagship congregation', in St John's Wood Road, London, with a series of events. An important distinction for them is that whereas traditional Jews insist on matrilineal descent, that is, if your mother is Jewish then you are Jewish, Liberal Jews are happy to call someone a Jew whose father is Jewish. Another significant characteristic is their inclusive attitude to gays and lesbians. They have been fellow campaigners with us and the Quakers for the right to hold civil partnership ceremonies in places of worship.

One relatively new Liberal Jewish group, called *Beit Klal Yisrael* (House for All Israel), was founded by a group of lesbian feminists, 'determined to create a Jewish community that welcomed and celebrated lesbian and gay life'. They have participated in Pride marches, the International Women's Day march, pre-Copenhagen Climate Change protest, an anti-Fascist - anti-EDL (English Defence League) rally and the women's Reclaim the Night rally.

And where does this group meet? Why, Essex Church, the home of Kensington Unitarians, of course.

*

Manchester's Liberal Jews have met regularly at Cross Street Unitarian Chapel for some years, very appreciative of the hospitality. At their rabbi's induction last November, the congregation included representatives of 'our fellow liberals in faith the Unitarians and Quakers', said their report.

The chair of their congregation told me one day how thrilled they were to have obtained their own sacred Torah scrolls, which form the focal point of their worship services. "In the past, for our High Holy Day services, we have had to borrow scrolls from another synagogue. Now at last we have our own!" she said, the joy evident in her face.

"That's wonderful," I said. "Tell me, just out of interest, where did you get these scrolls from?"

"Oh, we bought them on eBay!" she replied.

The last time I saw her she had joined *Roundelay*, the choir based at

Cross Street Chapel and was there among the sopranos at the Unitarian congregation's Easter Morning service.

*

Most of my Jewish friendships have been with Reform Jews, another first cousin once removed. One tit-bit picked up in an interfaith discussion is something I think we could use, if needed. We were talking about tradition, recognised as a powerful presence in Judaism, as those who have seen *Fiddler on the Roof* will remember. I quoted Garrison Keillor, a favourite writer, who, talking about his fictional creation, the very Christian town of Lake Wobegon, Minnesota, said of it, "It's a place where tradition is important, and sometimes all we have." I have pondered that a lot.

A response from a Reform Jew stuck in my mind, partly because of its anagrammatically memorable character. "Among Reform Jews," she said, "tradition has a vote, but not a veto."

*

Another anniversary this year is 190 years of the *Guardian,* which I still think of as the Unitarian newspaper. Founded by Unitarians, initially as a weekly, in response to the Peterloo Massacre, it has always stood aside from and often against conservative conventional wisdom, notably supporting votes for women, opposing the Boer war concentration camps and much more. Its famous editor, CP Scott, who held the post for over fifty years, was certainly a Unitarian. One of the current associate editors, Ian Mayes, is working on the next volume of the history of the paper, and has been looking into its Unitarian past. He has visited Essex Hall and Harris Manchester College and I enjoyed a friendly chat with him when he called in at Cross Street Chapel, which stands only a few yards from the original home of what was then called the *Manchester Guardian.* The name was changed when the office was moved to London.

He asked if I thought CP Scott's 1921 dictum, 'Comment is free, but facts are sacred', still held good. Not an easy question in these days of media spin. Facts are not easy to discern, so perhaps the dictum merits serious re-consideration. Maybe that is why the *Guardian* calls its blog, *Comment is Free…*

One *Manchester Guardian* piece, recently reproduced from an 1821 issue, described the grim scene of the public hanging of three criminals, one for robbery, one for burglary and "a youth, apparently about 17" for passing a forged £10 note. Shuddering at this, I ponder whether another, later slogan, much loved by Unitarians at one time but now more often derided, *The progress of mankind, onward and upward forever*, might have some truth in it after all. Not only would we today be outraged at such a grotesque punishment of a youngster for such a comparatively minor offence, we have progressed to the abolition of the death penalty altogether, with no sign of its return.

*

The aforementioned Cross Street Chapel enjoyed a neighbourly Palm Sunday lunchtime visit from the Very Rev. Rogers Govender, Dean of Manchester. A South African of Indian origin, he spoke of his experiences as a young priest in the apartheid era, recalling his appointments to parishes in both Durban and Pietermaritzburg, where the parsonages were in 'white' areas. To live there, as a black man, he was required to obtain a permit, a requirement with which he refused to comply.

As for experiences in city centre Manchester, he mentioned the St George's day event at the cathedral, which featured a large puppet depicting England's patron saint as a black man. There is, of course, a distinct possibility that George was not exactly white, being of Eastern Mediterranean extraction. However, this characterisation brought hate mail to the cathedral from far right political groups, not for the first time. With his South African experience, I'm sure the Dean dealt appropriately with that dragon.

July 2011

Cheque-books, tolerance and a cornucopia

The difficulties we grapple with regarding churchgoing in the present era are faced by most denominations. Keeping sufficient money flowing in and recruiting men and women to train for the ministry are just two problem areas. As for our religious principles, maintaining tolerance sometimes tests us. We are happy to learn from other tolerant religious groups, even those from the Orient.

Huw Thomas, our national treasurer, will surely be one of many treasurers heaving a sigh of relief at the decision made by the UK Payments Council, a somewhat mysterious body that sets policy on how banks pass our money around between themselves. It has decided to reprieve cheques. Bankers had deemed that this favourite way of handing over money would be abolished by 2018, calling on us all to go electronic. This conjured up nightmare visions of church treasurers everywhere passing those little gadgets along the pews every Sunday for worshippers to use as they try to remember their PIN numbers during the singing of the offertory hymn. Sure enough, the money managers at Unitarian Headquarters prefer to pay us electronically for routine expenses claims, but when it comes to donations, there is nothing quite like opening an envelope and seeing a cheque, seemingly smiling up at you. Folded neatly, they fit so nicely into those offertory envelopes that invite Gift Aid. The next best thing to real money, long live the cheque!

*

Are comparisons odious or helpful? When we wonder about the decline in organised religion does it help to see how other denominations are faring, or does it add to our anxiety? For my part I draw only a little comfort from the thought that the Church of England Synod has been agonising over statistics of decline, the *Baptist Times* has made yet another call for more evangelism and the Roman Catholic Church in Britain faces a crisis in recruitment to the priesthood. Priests are labouring on well past any conventional retirement age and congregations are being merged, even in areas with high church-going levels. Is it because of the child abuse allegations? I'm not sure, but for recruitment to the ministry, it means that it isn't just us having a thin time. Indeed it may be statistically possible to show that we are doing better than the RCs. Perhaps that's to do with our willingness to recruit women.

*

Some churches however are growing apace. A handsome, former court-house building stands empty in Skipton, a 'lion and the unicorn' emblem above the door, with *Dieu et Mon Droit* in gold letters (A wag once told me this means *My God, I'm Right!*). A notice tells me that application has been made for change of use, to a place of worship for the Church of Jesus Christ of Latter Day Saints, commonly known as the Mormons. I can lodge objections at the Town Hall, if I wish.

I have twice in recent years found myself in deep conversation with young men from committed Mormon families (they are great believers in 'the family'), who had even served their requisite stint as missionaries. Along the way they had become aware of this family-oriented church's distinctly negative attitude towards homosexuality, which had led them to the painful realisation that they didn't belong there any longer.

Should I register an objection to this courthouse change of use? Unitarian tolerance forbids me from trying to ban their doctrines, but what about their social justice views? Now comes news of a musical show called *The Book of Mormon*, on its way from Broadway to the UK. It is apparently a rollicking, bawdy, not to say outrageous send-up of Mormonism and all its ways. Tolerance is being tested. Will there be protest demos in our streets? Who can say 'My God I'm Right' here?

*

The 150th anniversary of the birth of Rabindranath Tagore is attracting interest in the national press, much of it complaining about how badly neglected Tagore is. No mention of any Unitarian connection, or the fact that some of his prayers and poems have been used by us for generations. The nearest we get is recognition of Tagore as a founder of the Brahmo Somaj movement. We are, however, well ahead of the field in marking this anniversary, the Honorary Governors and Friends of Harris Manchester College having had a lecture on him from the leading authority on Tagore's language and literature, William Radice. This was in June 2010, which was the 80th anniversary of Tagore's 1930 visit to the College to deliver the Hibbert Lectures, which he did to a packed Arlosh Hall, then gave the address on Sunday in a packed College chapel.

William Radice's lecture appears in *Faith and Freedom* (Autumn/Winter 2010). How was this scoop achieved? Radice has close connections with Unitarians. His wife is a former head of Channing School, he is an Honorary Governor of HMCO, has used the library there for research and has also written some hymns, one of which appears in *Hymns of Faith and Freedom*. Keith Gilley, retiring editor of *Faith and Freedom* tells me that this is the only hymn he has ever come across with the word 'cornucopia' in it.

August 2011

Retirees, rioters and a martyr

In August 2011, thousands of people rioted in London and several other towns and cities, resulting in looting, arson and the death of five people. The disturbances began after a protest, following the death of a man who was shot by police. Other towns and cities in England suffered what was described by the media as copycat violence. Ultimately more than a thousand people were issued with criminal charges for various related offences. City centre Manchester was affected. Rev. Jane Barraclough was minister there at that time but died some months later following a series of illnesses.

Yorkshire seems to be a favoured place for retired Unitarian ministers. Ernest Baker has decided to stay there after his retirement. Margaret Kirk shows no sign of moving elsewhere and Andrew Hill headed there when he left Scotland. Celia and I were next to settle, soon followed by Bill Darlison from Dublin. John and Beryl Allerton have a bolt-hole in the county, to which they frequently escape. It seems probable that Paul Travis, for whom retirement is only a few months away, will stay there too, and Brian and Kathy Packer have moved there from the south of England. It may all be simply co-incidence, of course, or perhaps affordability of property explains the trend.

*

Another recent member of the ranks of the retired to choose Yorkshire is former Unitarian minister, Duncan McGuffie. After brief ministries in the 1970s, first in our High Pavement Chapel, Nottingham, then Bournemouth, he left us for the Church of England. He settled for some years as parish priest in Clavering (the name means 'place of clover', which could invite a comment!). I was glad to join Ernest Baker and meet up with Duncan for lunch not long ago, and, in case you are wondering, the event bore no resemblance to Yorkshire-based *Last of the Summer Wine*. His jovial company and witty conversation remain undiminished.

Duncan McGuffie drawn by Rod Dixon

Duncan keeps in touch with our movement through the Old Students' Association at Manchester College, Oxford where he trained. He is perhaps best remembered for a useful booklet, *The Hymn Sandwich: A Brief History of Unitarian Worship*, published over thirty years ago by the then Worship Sub-Committee. It has this delightful caricature on its cover, produced by another former Unitarian minister, Rod Dixon. I can report that the real Duncan still looks very like the picture.

*

In a previous column I made mention of the murder, by racists, of UU minister Rev. James Reeb, on a Civil Rights march in Selma, Alabama in 1965. The perpetrators of this killing were never convicted, though I had learned that the case was being re-investigated. Alas, the news now is that this matter has been dropped. A note in the *Guardian* newspaper reads, "Five years ago the FBI set up a special unit to look at cold cases, but already the agency has admitted defeat in 60 of them. The task is made more difficult with every month that passes as key witnesses and suspects die." Presumably the James Reeb case is one of those abandoned, a sad outcome for his family, friends, colleagues, and indeed for us all, as well as for Justice.

*

The morning after the night of the August riots, I was holidaymaking near Manchester so headed for the city centre to see the aftermath for myself. On the Metro tram the conversation was predictably angry, blaming parents, schools, lack of discipline *etc,* plus one man's proposal to re-introduce transportation as a punishment, not to Australia this time but to another planet. "They don't belong on this one!" was his verdict. The city centre was strangely quiet, but with the unusual sound coming from brooms and brushes, as young volunteers swept up broken glass. Some had 'I ♥ Manchester' painted on their faces. I didn't ask where they were from, but I'm sure it was this planet.

*

Next stop was the Wednesday lunchtime service in Cross Street Chapel. "I've abandoned the theme I had prepared for today, obviously," said Rev. Jane Barraclough with a smile. We shared thirty minutes of quietness, calm words and lovely piano music from Cody Coyne, who commences training for our ministry in October. We sang 'I'll bring you hope, when hope is hard to find' (*Sing Your Faith* 24). Candles of concern were lit, for the healing of our 'two nations', and in thanksgiving that the Chapel offers a spiritual oasis in the heart of a riotous city. In the silence I recalled that the last time I had been aware of boisterous activity around here was in witnessing the fun of the Pride march, and before that, the singing and dancing street entertainment that accompanied the 2002 Commonwealth Games.

*

As you read this next paragraph, many questions may well pop into your mind. I'll tell you in advance that my answer to all of them is, "I don't know." I called in at the little newsagent's shop near the Chapel and chatted to the sole (Asian) shopkeeper. "Yes, the police have asked us to close early today in case rioting starts again," he said. "It's the looting."

"Well, I hope it's all over now," I responded and made to leave. Just then, a group of eight young teenage boys came in, all wearing the now notorious hoodies (though not over their faces). I felt I could not just leave the man to deal with this alone, so I stood near the door and watched them. Two of the youngsters picked up drinks from a shelf and paid at the counter. The rest just shuffled around other parts of the shop. I stood my ground, watching and waiting until they eventually left. I waved 'cheerio' to the shop assistant and he beamed a great smile back at me as I headed back to the Metro.

As I said, I don't know…. except that I'm sure that they, too, were from this planet. We may not like a lot that happens on it, but this is the only one inhabited, as far as we know.

September 2011

Perhaps UUA leader needs a 'herogram'

Our co-religionists in the US are far more likely to become active in political issues than we are. The observations here reminded us of the differing meanings of the word 'universalist', and noted the early signs of difficult issues regarding migrants in Calais.

Our spiritual sisters and brothers in the US are celebrating the 50th anniversary of the coming together of the American Unitarian Association and the Universalist Church of America, and all the signs are that they regard the 1961 merger as a success. In the UK we are less familiar with the Universalist side, mainly because as a denomination it was never as widespread here as it was in the US. There are still some who rather simplistically believe that a Universalist is one who holds that all the world's religions are basically the same. The original meaning, however, centres on the affirmation that eternal salvation through Christ is available to all, not simply the chosen few. This was heresy in its day.

*

One element of the Universalist Church that survives independently is 'the oldest continuously published liberal religious magazine in North America', *The Universalist Herald*. The Spring 2011 issue has an article which points out that the current Pope, Benedict 16th, could fairly be called a universalist, and this is not just because the word 'catholic' means universal. On Christmas Eve 2010 Pope Benedict gave the Thought for the Day on BBC Radio 4, in which he proclaimed Christ as the saviour of all people throughout the world and throughout history. No mention of 'the chosen few' (saved) or those 'outside the church' (doomed). The Universalist stance, it seems, has at long last been vindicated.

*

Indeed, it is hard to find a theologian of repute prepared to stand by a firm belief that some souls will be damned for all eternity. Even Karl Barth, usually regarded as an arch-conservative, was accused of being a universalist, a charge he never refuted. The thought that in the end everyone is saved has raised the question as to whether Adolf Hitler is in heaven. It makes an interesting discussion topic, as well as an introduction to Universalism. Then again, as Mark Twain said, "I don't like to commit myself about heaven and hell - you see, I have friends in both places."

*

Intriguing to learn that current UUA president, Rev. Peter Morales, was convicted in August on misdemeanor charges stemming from his non-violent civil disobedience in Phoenix, Arizona, in July 2010. He was arrested while protesting against Arizona's anti-immigrant legislation, SB 1070 : "My decision to engage in civil disobedience last July was rooted in my profound opposition to Arizona's SB 1070 and to the inhumane practices of Maricopa County Sheriff Joe Arpaio," he said. "My conviction as a result of that civil disobedience in no way alters my commitment to opposing this legislation that targets and dehumanizes some of the most vulnerable among us." I enjoyed a friendly chat with Peter at an international Ministers' conference in Holland, just a couple of weeks before his protest. I'm no expert but he didn't have the look of a criminal protestor to me. Perhaps that's why he got to serve only one day in jail.

Have we ever had a GA President in jail? Anybody seen Ann Peart lately?

*

The word 'herogram' is new to me. It is a letter telling you what a great job you have done. Following the uproar about phone hacking and the demise of the *News of the World* (no great loss, say I) the *Guardian* has been on the receiving end of plaudits for its excellent journalism in exposing the outrage. A few of these were published, but, "The letters page was dominated by a flood of letters commenting on and arguing about the many issues raised by the developing scandal.... but we kept the herograms for internal consumption (sticking them on the office wall) in line with the reticence of our Unitarian founders, who would undoubtedly have frowned at such frivolous excesses," says *Guardian* letters editor Nigel Willmott. So, our Unitarian forbears are remembered for their reticence regarding their virtues.

Are we still? I do my best.

*

A brief holiday in Normandy was most enjoyable, giving us a taste of real summer weather. An unexpected treat was watching people dancing in the street, something I always enjoy and find somehow reassuring. Some Unitarians will be familiar with the prayer that includes, "May the skies be clear, and may the streets be safe...". Safe enough in Rouen, it seems, for salsa dancing, something I had heard of but never seen before. At one point, a police car cruised by for a look, hovered for a while and then drifted off, the occupants presumably deciding that it was a benign, warm summer evening activity. All ages, races and levels of ability were joining in, many with serious looks on their faces as it requires some concentration, but undoubtedly having fun, and certainly not rioting.

*

By contrast, an experience on the journey home left me feeling troubled. The otherwise speedy and comfortable Eurostar train broke down at Calais, mercifully before we had entered the Channel tunnel. Everybody out, on to the platform for a two-hour wait, bottled water and crisps passed around to keep us a little refreshed. After a few minutes I realised that Calais station was completely caged in, with high fencing all around. There were armed soldiers pacing up and down nearby, presumably watching out for illegal migrants. The presence of soldiers with guns always makes me feel more nervous, when their task, I suppose, is to make me feel secure. I feel the same about armed policemen, as I come from a lost generation when there were none to be seen, ever. The fact that one of these soldiers was a woman made it even more troubling, though I am not sure why. It was by no means as objectionable a scenario as that faced by Peter Morales in Arizona, but I still didn't like it, though not enough to protest and be sent to jail, not even for one day.

October 2011

Perhaps a Professor of Unitarian Studies?

As well as noting the activities of other denominations, we like to have a look at ourselves, both in the UK and North America and, in this instance, South Africa. We also enjoy noting how others see us, especially as we often feel ignored or neglected.

A further recent encounter with Quakers brings me up to date with their journals and a chance to compare theirs with ours. Like us, they have two. Both current issues are more expensive than the *Inquirer* and are largely in colour. This is unusual and it is because they are special issues for 'Quaker Week', an annual event when they throw all their energies into outreach.

"How did you enjoy your Yearly Meeting," I asked one attender, who had been a delegate to their equivalent to our denominational Annual Meetings.

"All a bit overwhelming for a first-timer like me," she replied, "but very good."

"Anything exciting or controversial on the agenda?" I asked.

"We've gone green. It was all about the environment, reducing our carbon footprint and all that. But then, there was a *load* of paperwork produced about it. Must have been half a forest!" she added ruefully.

So the Quakers have their problems getting things just right, too, especially with an attendance at their annual gathering much larger than ours.

*

Quaker News contained a name that leapt off the page at me. Birmingham University has a Professor of Quaker Studies (albeit an honorary one). He also teaches at Woodbrooke, their sumptuous study centre based in the former home of Quaker chocolate maker George Cadbury. In addition, he has a growing list of publications to his name, which is Professor Ben Pink Dandelion.

Yes, it is. Look it up.

Ah, would that we had a Professor of Unitarian Studies somewhere. Anyone care to put forward a name?

*

Spring has arrived in South Africa where our Unitarian community appears to be growing apace. In the past there was the main congregation in Cape Town, plus an offshoot group in nearby Somerset West. There is a long established fellowship in Johannesburg and another in Durban. Now there are more. Since his retirement, Rev. Gordon Oliver has been leading a new fellowship he began a couple of years ago at Fish Hoek, down the coast a little from Cape Town. This I recall as a wonderful place to go penguin-spotting, then whale-watching, then gaze southwards out across the ocean and ponder that the next stop is Antarctica. No Unitarians there, as far as I know, though Rev. Andrew

Hill's ornithologist son Christopher at one time worked there with the British Antarctic Survey. More recently, present Cape Town minister Rev. Roux Malan has started an Afrikaans speaking group on the north side of the city. My knowledge of that language is non-existent, but reading their advertisement I discern that this is an 'Afrikaanse satellietgroep', and I am encouraged by the words 'Verwelkoming' and 'Koffie en Klets', when a little research tells me 'klets' is their word for chat, as used for their 'chat' lines. Visitors are always made very welcome.

*

The Unitarian Renewal Group is a sort of ginger-group, and its October Day Gathering in Bradford gave opportunity for predictions as to what the Unitarian movement might be up to in the year 2020 with speculations by Andrew Hill, Stephen Lingwood and Yvonne Aburrow. This kind of crystal ball-gazing has been tried before. A sample of a previous effort, penned by Howard Hague in 2000, was read out. It included predictions that by 2025 we would be having a world gathering of Unitarians in front of computer screens and that our headquarters would have moved to Cross Street Chapel, Manchester. Perhaps more accurately it predicted Unitarian groups emerging in South America. Indeed, there are already groups to be found in Mexico, Cuba, Puerto Rico, Bolivia, Brazil and Argentina. The Argentina contacts include an enthusiast in Tierra del Fuego, not so far from Antarctica after all.

*

In September, the *Guardian's* online version gave us a sort of off-beat look at 'how others see us'. Journalist Theo Hobson described his experience of visiting a Unitarian service in Brooklyn, New York. He went along as a complete newcomer and he came away with the conclusion that, "Unitarianism carries about as much sense of dangerous otherness as a tots sing-along at the local library." The article was accompanied by a picture of Newington Green Chapel, not in New York but here in London, so it was no surprise to see, in the ensuing correspondence, a robust rejoinder from Rev. Andy Pakula, Newington Green and Islington minister. He pointed out that Unitarians have faced plenty of danger in their time, citing the martyr Michael Servetus, burned alive as a heretic in October 1553, as well as many others since who have faced danger and death.

Whether this exchange of views has attracted anyone to go along to a Unitarian place of worship, I don't know. Many other responses were from more evangelical sources, some of them quite strident. So it was good to spot a little humour among the vitriol. Commenting on the Unitarian insistence on 'The One', a respondent wrote, "That reminded me of the old Les Dawson joke: 'There's a tribe in Africa that worships the number zero. Is nothing sacred?'"

November 2011

Wobegon in Boston, stir-up Sunday

I enjoy keeping up with the work of my alma mater, Unitarian College, watching the progress of students and observing the changes in their training and education. Similarly, the interest that Celia and I have in international denominational activities gives opportunities for overseas visits to experience the challenge of differences as well as the joys of similarities and friendships.

Driving to the Unitarian College Governors' Autumn Meeting, I listened to news reports about the financial problems in Greece. Economics usually leaves me bewildered. Where has all the money gone, and why? In the Governors' Meeting, money matters were again to the fore and my ears pricked up when I heard the word 'Greek' again. The College's money managers have decided to amalgamate some of its many trust funds in the interests of simplification. One of these provides the Bibby Prize for Proficiency in Greek, now deemed obsolete. I was almost tempted to speak out against this move, recalling (to my own surprise, I admit) that I had been a recipient of this prize in my final year at the College in the mid-1960s. The disappearance of such an award says something about the changing expectations, education and the training of ministers, who nowadays are more likely to be proficient, not in ancient languages but in organisational management, or even economics, and that's all Greek to me!

*

There followed a talk from Dr Graham Johnston, in charge of the Unitarian College archives at the renowned John Rylands Library in Manchester. He read out a letter from one of the earliest (mid-19th century) applicants to train for the ministry at UCM, and we laughed to hear the applicant describe himself as a 'druggist'. The word had a different meaning then, but linked with the word 'student', it gave an amusing impression to 21st century listeners. This brought back to my mind a scurrilous thought I once entertained, that of posing the question, 'Which former UCM Principal was a drug-addict?' The answer would have been the much admired scholar-minister Alexander Gordon, who became Principal in 1890. Herbert McLachlan's biography of Alexander Gordon tells that he was an habitual taker of snuff, which he purchased by the pound! An addiction? Sounds like it to me, though this is disputed. Pope Urban VIII (1568–1644) ordered that anyone found guilty of taking snuff in church should be excommunicated. Perhaps that's why the staunch Non-Subscribing Presbyterian Alexander Gordon favoured it.

*

Boston Massachusetts ranks high among my favourite cities, so I leapt at a chance of a visit, while my wife Celia joined in meetings of the Executive Committee of the International Council of Unitarians and Universalists. I strolled on Boston Common and the Public Gardens, the leaves red, yellow and gold, the Autumn sunshine, warm even in November, glinting on the Make Way for Ducklings sculpture, adored by children of all ages. People were friendly and helpful. Trips on the T, the robust and efficient subway trains, took me to excellent museums and galleries. The city is blessed with three central UU churches within a half mile of each other, all alive, in business and with more than one minister each. We were welcomed at worship at Kings Chapel and at First Church, two very different experiences. Ah, to be in a country where church-going is the norm for a far higher percentage of the population than in the UK. Who can tell me why?

*

It was sad, however, to see homeless and rootless people on the city's streets, asking for "spare change", dossing in doorways, the parks and subway stations. At all three worship services we attended, we prayed for those affected badly by the present economic crisis.

*

A Sunday afternoon birthday treat was a one-man performance at Boston Symphony Hall by Garrison Keillor, of whom I have been a fan for many years. He talked and occasionally sang, uninterrupted for over two hours, mostly about his (fictional) home town of Lake Wobegon, Minnesota, "where all the women are strong, all the men are good looking and all the children are above average." Everyday stuff on first hearing, yet he simultaneously amuses and touches the depths. It was like a long, engaging sermon. "The thing that people here fear the most is that when they die they will be remembered for the most stupid thing they ever did in their lives." He hints at the hopes and concerns of the church-goers, young and old, and their clergy, mainly Lutheran or 'Sanctified Brethren', though occasionally Unitarians get a mention. "We don't go in much for tolerance or non-denominationalism," he once wrote. "In the Bible we don't find the word 'maybe' so much, or where God says, 'Well, er, there may be more than one way of looking at this.' So, we go in for strict truth, and let the other guy be tolerant of us." His radio programme, *A Prairie Home Companion* has been running weekly for years all over the US. Many of his books and tapes are available and an inexhaustible delight.

*

We stayed as guests of UU minister Robert Walsh and his wife Kitty. Robbie has undertaken retirement ministries in the UK and Australia and now lives in Hingham where they attend the renowned Old Ship Church. He is perhaps best known for the delightful *Noisy Stones* (1991)

27

one of the best of the long-running stream of excellent Skinner House meditation manuals. Current GA President Ann Peart tells me she has used this one in services up and down the land, so she and others will be pleased to learn that he has a second volume out, *Stone Blessings* (2010) with more gems. I relish especially his hilarious revelation of the last thing he habitually did each Sunday morning, the moment before entering the chapel in Duxbury Massachusetts, where he served as minister. He would take out his gown and swing it dramatically around his shoulders and say to himself, "This must be a job for Clergyman!" Robbie is not, however, a gentleman, at least not by Mark Twain's definition: "A gentleman knows how to play the banjo, and doesn't."

*

Home, then, just in time for Stir-up Sunday. My stirring-the-Christmas-pudding wishes were for all bankers to learn some morality to go with their economics and for good friend Robbie to keep on writing and playing the banjo and never mind about being a gentleman. Greetings to all ministers and church-goers, everywhere.

December 2011

2012

A banjo, an earthquake and toilets

2012

A banjo, an earthquake and toilets

Now, what do we do for Easter?

The start of a new year prompts a look back to the recent Christmas activities and a look ahead to Easter, Unitarians having mixed feelings and opinions about the main Christian festivals. Also, a brief book review and further thoughts about churchgoing, and not just ours.

"Have you recovered from Christmas?" a colleague once asked in January. I understood the question. It can be a strenuous and stressful time, but I gave a cheery reply as I always enjoy the festive season and refuse to be swamped by the commercialisation or beaten by the busyness. I reminded my colleague that our American cousins habitually refer to it all as 'holiday', and 'Happy holiday' is often heard as a greeting on their side of the Atlantic, but not ours. "Doesn't feel much like a holiday to me," was the reply. In the UK we are far more likely to use that word for our summer holiday, when Americans use the word 'vacation'. Truth to tell, our US cousins have probably got it right, as

Christmas, strictly speaking, should be perceived as a 'holy day', where-as in summer we 'vacate' our homes and workplaces.

*

I usually try to avoid all the so-called 'humorous' greetings cards, dislik-ing the ageism, sexism and banality that is usually to be found in them. This last December, however, I spotted one in WH Smith's that amused me with its not too irreverent quirkiness. It's by cartoonist Jamie Charteris. The scene is a castle where the Three Kings are setting the table for Christmas dinner, turkey and all the trimmings. Through the window, guests can be seen arriving up the driveway, namely Mary, bear-ing a gift and Joseph pushing the bobble-hatted infant Jesus in a buggy. One of the Kings is explaining to a servant, "Last year we went to them. So, this year they are coming to us!"

*

Next major Christian festival to come up is Easter, one we do refer to as a 'holiday'. Is Easter more holy than Christmas? Unitarians often struggle with it. I recall a conversation with a primary school teacher in which I asked what she usually tells her children about the Easter story. "We're advised to avoid it altogether," she said. "Stick to bunnies and Easter eggs." Not long ago the Unitarian Renewal Group presented a session at the GA Annual Meetings under the title, *What Did You Do for Easter?* In the ensuing discussion, there was a gasp of astonishment when one speaker reported that at his church the congregation had duly turned up, none of them knowing that it was Easter Sunday at all until someone arrived with an Easter egg to share. Sure enough, the Christian doctrines that explain the meaning of the Crucifixion and Resurrection do not resonate much with Unitarians, it seems to me. Simon Hoggart in the *Guardian* reported recently that someone had told him about a wayside pulpit with the words, 'Either Jesus paid, or you do'. The best response he could come up with was, "Well, at least it assumes some knowledge of the doctrine of the atonement."

*

Help is at hand for Yorkshire Unitarians. A notice told me that their January District quarterly meeting will be preceded by a session for their lay preachers. The topic will be a sharing of ideas and approaches to Easter in Unitarian worship; an open session for all to share thoughts and ideas. The event was held at Hull, one of a few of our congregations which have alms-houses connected. Not physically attached, but with an all-Unitarian board of trustees managing a substantial endowment, providing accommodation for the elderly. York Unitarians have something similar. Hull's responsibility is the Leonard Chamberlain Trust, which dates from the early eighteenth century. After a recent visit there I enjoyed reading a new history of the trust. Decades ago, as a student for the ministry, I was pleased to learn that this trust includes money for educational purposes and I was sent off for an interview by the trustees, as a result of which I received a very useful book grant. Searching through the history book for the relevant item in the terms of the trust which would show that I had qualified for this grant, I came across this from about 1720: '£10 towards the education or maintenance of a scholar for four years at some academy or other in England or Scotland, one of a pregnant wit, of a ready speech and hopeful for godliness and piety.'

Hmm. I hope they don't ever ask for their money back.

*

It always bothers me slightly when I read the list of best-selling books for the closing year, as I usually find I haven't read any of them. This year-end, however, I was pleased to spot *The Help*, by Kathryn Stockett which I have enjoyed, if enjoy is the word I want. Most reviewers commented on the funny bits, but I was deeply affected by the women's perspective on racism, as experienced by African Americans in Deep South Mississippi in the 1960s. The experience of prejudice becomes especially sensitive when it comes to cleaning bedrooms and lavatories and bringing up other people's children. Read it when you are feeling strong.

*

The 31 December issue of *The Guardian* contained a *Face to Faith* column from Pope Benedict, which included something I had not seen before from a Roman Catholic source, an admission of decline: "…regular churchgoers are growing older all the time and their number is constantly diminishing; …recruitment of priests is stagnating; …scepticism and unbelief are growing. What, then, are we to do? There are endless debates over what must be done in order to reverse the trend."

*

CM: What are you looking at now?

JM. The New Year's Honours list. I'm searching for Unitarians.

CM. Anything interesting?

JM. No, but I've just seen that someone got an honour for services to beekeeping in Surrey.

CM. Well, bees *are* under threat.

JM. So are Unitarians, and Roman Catholics, if the Pope's views are anything to go by.

January 2012

Maybe we need to be a bit more like Beryl

Always expect the unexpected is a valuable slogan to adopt. We easily fall into the trap of stereotyping. So, just as we dislike it when others misunderstand us, so we should beware of misjudging others, be they entertainers, schoolchildren or compilers of dictionaries.

As a student I borrowed (all right, plagiarised) a sermon idea from the great American Liberal Christian preacher, Harry Emerson Fosdick: *Finding God in Unlikely Places.* The notion has stuck with me, so I was glad to have my attention drawn by comedian Mark Steel to a story about George Formby (1904-1961), who enjoyed enormous popularity as an entertainer in the 1930s and 40s, especially in the north of England. His statue stands in his home town of Wigan and another on the Isle of Man. A brilliant ukulele-banjo player, George also starred in films, usually as a likeable, innocent abroad character. Some of his songs, replete with *double-entendres*, were banned by the BBC, though he was a popular entertainer of the troops during WW2.

In the late 1940s he toured South Africa in pre-apartheid days, refused to play to segregated audiences and gave no less than twenty free concerts in black African townships, much to the consternation of government officials. At one of these shows, he gave a hug to a little black girl after she had presented his wife with a box of chocolates. This was too much for Dr Daniel Malan, who later became the Nationalist Party prime minister who introduced apartheid. He phoned George to chide him for such "despicable stunts". George's feisty, not to say formidable wife Beryl took the call, and responded, "Why don't you p*ss off, you 'orrible little man!"

George Formby a radical social justice campaigner? I love it!

*

I am also pleased to spot 'Unitarian' in unexpected places. A *Guardian* cryptic crossword recently had: *'Nun oddly including it with song of religious group'* (9). The compiler, 'Brendan', was born in Ireland but now lives in the US. I have memories of someone once suggesting that we should contrive to get our name in as many crosswords as possible, as a subtle form of free publicity. Has anyone ever become a Unitarian along such a route? There have been stranger and more unlikely ways.

*

I enjoyed a *Guardian* article about Gooderstone Primary school in Norfolk. It places strong emphasis on SEAL, i.e. Social and Emotional Aspects of Learning. The school's policies and staff attitudes stress the importance of the happiness of the children, even their involvement in decision making on matters that affect their happiness. By contrast, government policies are moving away from such supposedly nebulous thoughts and describe SEAL as "ghastly", and "likely to distract from the core subjects of academic education." The official move now is towards 'universal standards' and 'norms', rather than individual growth and happiness. I was particularly taken with the report that the school's head teacher, David Baldwin, "recently asked pupils what they thought of assembly, and while one girl appreciated the chance to 'talk to God', everyone wanted to be the one to blow out the assembly candle." Has someone sneaked a little Unitarian influence in there? Is the 'assembly candle' at all like our flaming chalice? Better keep quiet about it, I fear. If it gets too popular, health and safety legislators might follow hard on the heels of those who don't particularly want our children to find happiness in school, and ban the candle-lighting. If so, we can only hope that parents send their youngsters along to the GA youth events led by John Harley and friends at Great Hucklow. The chalice will surely be lit there, amid plenty of SEAL.

*

Some years ago, fellow retiree Andrew Hill began to gather definitions or descriptions of Unitarianism from encyclopedias and dictionaries. He has quite a collection. Here's another he can add. While *Wikipedia*, the on-line free encyclopedia, became unavailable for a day in January (in protest over new US piracy legislation), I found my way to *Conservapedia*, the right-wing alternative. One always wonders where such resources get their information. This one doesn't much like the NHS, nor Barack Obama with his "socialism, Marxism and liberal policies." And what are we to make of:

> *Unitarians are religious liberals who stress the freedom of the individual to seek religious truth through the use of reason. Considering the dogma of the Trinity a corruption of Christianity, they believe in the unity of God and view Jesus as strictly human. The name Unitarian derives from this opposition to the Trinitarians. Unitarians accept Jesus as one of humanity's great teachers and generally hold an optimistic view concerning the ability of man (sic) to achieve his own salvation.*

So far, so good. But then we get:

> 'Unitarian churches are notable for their high turnover, as people move through briefly on their way into or out of Christianity.

Searching further, I found that there is also *Liberapedia*, a site that shares and promotes liberal views on the issues of the day. Their description of us includes:

> *A Unitarian is a liberal with weird feelings. Unitarians are about providing a community with some... spirituality for members with a wide range of beliefs.*

*

Unitarians seem to be a very well-behaved lot, whereas troublesome Quakers are in the news again. Eighty-two year old John Voysey of Ludlow Meeting is scheduled to appear in a magistrates' court for his boycott of the 2011 census. He will refuse to pay a fine and is willing to face prison. A conscientious objector since his youth, John's protest is over the fact that the £150 million contract for running the census in England was awarded to a division of Lockheed Martin, the world's largest armaments company. He refused to complete the census, which is technically an offence, and adds that if he paid the fine, he would become an accessory to the activities of the arms industry. Quaker journal, *The Friend* reports that, "Critics point out that thousands of people routinely ignore the census without facing prosecution. This time many boycotters returned their blank census forms with letters of protest." This makes prosecution easier so at least 400 could be on their way to court for it.

It seems to me that these days British Unitarians are being nudged toward being much more up-front on social justice issues, like the Quakers, or our American cousins. Will such behaviour increase our visibility and attract newcomers to join us? See you in court? Better not behave like Beryl Formby.

February 2012

Another Inquirer

Earthquake? Or the strings of compassion in the Philippines?

The International Council of Unitarians and Universalists was pleased to accept an invitation to hold a council meeting in the Philippines. This was Autumn in February, with lovely sunshine and an opportunity to view the delightful and dramatic countryside as well as the crowded towns and cities. Worship with small, struggling congregations in modest buildings with the simplest of facilities reminded us how wealthy we are.

First surprise was to discover that the Philippines daily newspaper is called *The Inquirer*. Our guide assured us that "it's not a bad paper but occasionally gets a bit sensationalist" (unlike our venerable UK Unitarian journal, I was tempted to say). I wondered if the International Council of Unitarians and Universalists might stir up a sensation, but the locals seemed to take us in their stride. We were more than seventy delegates and visitors from all five continents, there for a five day Council meeting plus conference that was a thrilling, non-stop learning experience.

Quite unconnected (I hope!) on the day of our arrival was an earthquake measuring 6.8, a few miles away. We made light of this until we learned of the death toll. The only immediate effect on us was the hasty departure of all our hotel kitchen staff, who, fearing a tsunami, fled to higher ground or dashed off to see that their homes and families were safe, leaving us un-catered for. Minibuses transported us to a nearby restaurant, however, and the problem was solved.

*

The staff returned next day to offer buffet-style meals beside our hotel's outdoor swimming pool, under a straw-roofed pavilion, amid the gently swaying coconut palms. We enjoyed blue skies and warm winds blowing white-topped waves gently in from the Pacific. Star-apples, jackfruit and roast bananas were a first for me for breakfast. If this sounds too idyllic for sturdy non-conformists, well, we were advised not to travel there without insect-repellent and *Imodium*, and to be prepared for rainfall "of biblical intensity", as Frederick Muir's intriguing book describes it. *Maglipay Universalist!* which translates as *Rejoice, Universalist!* (2001), tells the story of how Unitarian Universalists came to be in the Philippines. We loved our visit but the sound of coconuts clattering down on to our meeting room roof warned us to be wary of strolling beneath those palms.

*

The warm winds blowing brought to mind a hymn, beloved of nineteenth century missionaries who travelled to this part of the world to preach salvation. *From Greenland's icy mountains* has this notorious verse:

What though the spicy breezes blow soft o'er Ceylon's isle;
Though every prospect pleases, and only man is vile?
In vain with lavish kindness the gifts of God are strown;
The heathen in his blindness bows down to wood and stone.

It was composed by Reginald Heber (1783–1826), who, as a result of his zeal for missions, became Anglican bishop to Calcutta, India, where he was the first to ordain a Hindu to the ministry. He died at the age of forty-three. These days we are not averse to use of the word pagan, but even we demur at 'heathen', though it means only a person from the heath. Heber's first draft of the hymn had the word 'savage', but he agreed to amend it. It is a source of pride among Unitarians that this hymn has never appeared in any of our hymnals.

*

So I didn't look for 'blind heathens' or 'savages' in The Philippines. On the contrary, the experience generally was one of smiling, friendly, helpful people. Not that there was an absence of problems. Crossing city streets was terrifying, with frantic, klaxonic, all-day traffic jams, motorbikes with as many as five aboard including children and grandma on the luggage carrier at the back. No sign of safety helmets. There were hundreds of fearsome taxis and buses, with scant use of safety belts (and yes, I just coined that word klaxonic). So, not entirely paradise islands; I was shocked by the sight of armed guards at the doors of local shops and supermarkets. Not unconnected, I think, is the manifest gulf between rich and poor. The degree of affluence here is indicated by the height of security fences outside some suburban homes, though, come to think of it, that applies in the UK too. The strain of stretched family resources could perhaps be measured in the length of lines of washing outside poorer houses, some of them reminiscent of Appalachian mountain shacks, as in the film *Deliverance*. After a hotel meal in city centre Manila one evening, the waiter asked if we minded if he gave our left-overs to poor people outside on the street. Minded? *Minded!*

*

Philippine Unitarian Universalist churches are astonishing. Pre- and post-conference visits gave us the amazing sight of congregations consisting largely of children. Bicutan UU Community in Metro Manila is really a social service project, held under something resembling a near-derelict carport over a patch of unwanted land. We shuffled in to join a few adults and a couple of dozen cheery youngsters, one of whom, a girl aged twelve (yes, honestly) conducted the service with poise and assuredness. We all sang 'Spirit of Life' with greater feeling than I have heard in years, reading the words from a colourfully printed sheet stuck up on a breeze-block wall. I smiled at an intriguing typo as we sang of the 'strings of compassion' instead of the stirrings. My heart-strings were certainly touched when a delightful seven-year old girl gave me a paper heart (It was close to Valentine's Day) with her hand-written words that thanked me for coming. Thanked me? I was enthralled.

*

Nagbinlod is a country village out in the hills on a near-impassable road with rain-filled, crater-sized pot-holes. There is a UU sponsored mango plantation project next to a very humble, breeze-block, dirt floor church. The congregation, again mostly children, sang and danced for us to our utter delight. Sitting among them reminded me of the crowded Sunday schools of my boyhood, especially when I spotted 'somebody' loves 'somebody' scratched into the back of the wooden bench in front of me.

The work of blind heathens? No, more like the strings of compassion.

March 2012

All kinds of things that we cherish

Some concerns here about our heritage, illustrated by reports of the sale of church treasures. What is more important, precious silverware in the safe, or a restored building? Once it's gone, it's gone say the supermarkets offering bargains. Memories of a supportive former minister and delight at old-fashioned cinema-going, plus some humour in unexpected places, all point to more human treasures.

Harold MacMillan was Tory prime minister back in the so-called swinging sixties and is memorable for a number of phrases, including the one about "selling off the family silver". This was in a speech in 1985 in reference to the disposing of government assets and pretending this was income. The comparison was with a family in financial trouble. "First of all the silver goes; and then all that nice furniture that used to be in the salon; then the Canalettos go." I was reminded of these words when I learned that the UU congregation in Dorchester, Massachusetts recently sold its communion vessels and other silver items dating back to the 17th and 18th centuries, at Sotheby's in New York, for $1.7 million. The items sold included those donated to the church by members over the years, mostly in wills. "It was difficult for the congregation to [sell the silver], but we have a $5 million restoration project for our building," senior minister Arthur Lavoie said. He added, "The congregation realized that if we didn't act soon to do this work, we wouldn't be able to save the building. And the building is more important than the silver." In recent years other UU congregations have done something similar. A number of our UK congregations possess highly valuable items, and I'll never forget the wide-eyed look on the face of Rev. Cliff Reed when he appeared on the *Antiques Road Show* with the Ipswich Meeting House communion vessels and was told their value. Can we imagine any of our congregations selling off treasures like these?

*

Our local cinema is a delight. No 'multiplex studio', this is a good, old fashioned, independent picture house, with squashy seats and pleated curtains that are raised and lowered by an audibly groaning electric motor. An usher sells ice-cream from a tray in the interval as we sit on the back row, watching old Pearl and Dean adverts. Recent offerings have included *The Iron Lady*, too soft-centered, I think, to tell much about the real Margaret Thatcher, despite an Oscar-winning performance by Meryl Streep. The problem of aging was dealt with much better in *Iris* [2001], with the BAFTA-winning Judi Dench. *The Best Exotic Marigold Hotel,* again with Judi Dench, was also good on aging, and very entertaining, despite a little stereotyping. This picture house was an ideal place to see the Oscar-winning *The Artist*, a remarkably realistic trip down memory lane to the silent movies of the 1920s. The story is filled with simple vices of pride, stubbornness and unwillingness to change, and the equally simple virtues of loyalty, faithfulness and the love that conquers all. Some people used to preach sermons like that.

Happy days.

*

Sad to learn of the death of Keith Treacher, who was an influence on me and other young Unitarians back in the 1950s. I recall a very kind letter he wrote to encourage me on my way to Unitarian College to train for the ministry, and my sadness when he himself left it. He is the only person I ever met who refused to buy Mazda electric light bulbs (a brand no longer available) as he felt it would be offensive to members of the Parsee faith. For them, Ahura Mazda is the god of wisdom and light, hence the choice of the name. "I wonder what Christians might think if they saw 'Jesus Christ' light bulbs on sale, as Christ is the light of the world?" he asked. Thoughts about the apparent trivialisation, implying lack of respect for matters that others hold as sacred, came into my mind when I learned of complaints from the Buddhist Centre in Manchester, some years ago. They were about depictions of the Buddha used as the decor of a trendy bar in the city centre, where alcohol (and who knows what other substance) was consumed. I took the point and avoided the place, not that it was my kind of haunt anyway. Only recently, in a local shop, I saw a decidedly tacky statuette of a 'Lucky Buddha' for sale. Lucky? Since when did the quest for enlightenment have anything to do with luck? I didn't buy one, nor am I likely to patronise that shop. Did Keith Treacher make me over-sensitive?

*

Thoughts of the difficulties around depictions of important religious figures reminds me of the time, some years ago, when the GA Religious Education Department (of blessed memory) collaborated with the GA Publicity Department (also of blessed memory) and produced the first Unitarian Travelling Display. It consisted of a set of display boards, one of which had a picture of Jesus. Someone at the time rather cheekily said that the image looked more like Mick Jagger. Since then I have been keeping an eye out for a picture of Jesus that would suit

Unitarians, as we endeavour to keep to the GA Object, to 'uphold the Liberal Christian tradition'. All I have ever seen have either been of sweetly sentimental 'gentle Jesus', or of the supernatural 'sacred heart' Christ. None that I have seen portray a radical rabbi.

*

I have enjoyed friendships with a number of rabbis over the years, and most of them have been blessed with what is thought of as a Jewish sense of humour, something recognisable but difficult to define. None, however, were as amusing as Jackie Mason, rabbi-turned-comedian with a delightful New Yorker (or should I say 'Noo Yoiker') Jewish accent. A recent castaway on *Desert Island Discs*, he spiced up his life story with some characteristic gags. When asked about sushi, he said, "It's crazy. Nobody ate raw fish until they called it sushi. Somebody says to you, 'Have a piece of fish, I forgot to cook it,' what would you think? I reckon it was invented by two Jews who wanted to open a restaurant without a kitchen!" His willingness to tell seemingly anti-Jewish jokes puts me on edge, a little. I once attended the induction service of a Reform rabbi who came out with a remark that brought roars of laughter from the congregation, but left me wondering whether it was all right for me to laugh, or not. In his installation address he mentioned that one project he had been appointed to lead was a major fund-raising drive for the synagogue. "That's all right by me," he said. "There is nothing in this world gives me greater pleasure than getting money out of Jews!" I think I might use that one some time, but make it all right by saying 'Unitarians' instead.

April 2012

Co-op Sunday marked, now save Wedgwood

Some titbits of our history, but with affordable shopping from the Co-op stores and, by contrast, the luxuries of Wedgwood ceramics, all at risk. Some ministers who took risks with seemingly illicit activities both in the UK and overseas remind us that even our liberal and tolerant religion has its dangers.

Can you remember your Co-op number? This is the UN Year of Cooperatives, so it was appropriate for Rochdale Unitarians to mark

Co-operative Sunday, May 13, with a special service. There are co-operatives of various kinds worldwide, demonstrating that competitive capitalism is not the only way to do business. A first Co-op movement in Britain began in Toad Lane, Rochdale in 1844, with considerable Unitarian input. Our original Clover Street Chapel was known as 'the Co-op chapel'. I hope the commemorative service included a ritual chanting of Co-op numbers, as a remarkable number of people, me included, can remember theirs. It's the only bit of institutional brainwashing of which I can approve. A family legend tells that my mother once wrote to my brother in the army and put her Co-op number on the envelope instead of his regimental number. Fortunately, he recognised it when it was called out and, red-faced, collected his letter. Older readers will recall that not only did Co-op shops and businesses offer more affordable goods and services, there was the excitement of 'divi day', an annual dividend pay-out under the profit-sharing scheme.

*

My boyhood local Co-op had a central till, towards which cash payments whizzed in a brass tubular container along wires. Change came back the same way. Co-op shops persist, though the Co-op number has been replaced with a plastic card, like the supermarkets' club card. There are also Co-op banks, insurance services, travel agents and more, but one doesn't get 'divi' from Co-op Funeral Services. Good, affordable funeral arrangements are for everyone, but the thought of one's profit share being enhanced by the demise of a beloved family member is deemed a little unworthy.

*

Alas my local Co-op shop has just closed down, allegedly because its lease has expired, though suspicion falls on the proximity of two giant supermarkets. Once a large Co-op department store, it has progressively reduced to just a grocery and that has now closed, much to the particular chagrin of pensioner shoppers. It was close to the bus station, smaller and more user-friendly than the supermarkets. Next to the grocery section stood the Post Office, with a row of chairs available for those queuing for their pensions, a few stamps, perhaps, and a neighbourly moan that a first class stamp now costs 60p (that's twelve shillings!). Now the Post Office has closed and amid fears that it may be lost for ever. However, it is to re-open in a nearby disused pub, one of hundreds nationally that have closed in recent years. Is some sort of domino effect happening to community-friendly institutions? Pubs close down, small shops disappear, Post Offices are reduced in number. Some good news is that our local library has been reprieved. I certainly added my signature to the protest that included Alan Bennett's claim that closing down public libraries amounts to child abuse.

*

The struggle to maintain small, local organisations makes me reflect again on the difficulties in keeping congregations going. At the Annual Meetings in Keele I raised a question about that to our guest and Keynote Speaker, Paul Parker, senior staff member from Friends House, headquarters of the Quakers. They too agonise when any of their Meeting Houses closes down. Paul tentatively suggested that organisations have a life span, just as human beings do, and we should expect and accept that they will one day come to a natural end. I might find that acceptable if I could discern more clearly whether that ending had come, or not. Some congregations last for centuries, some just a few years. Who really knows why? I recall one congregation that had a quota membership of 40-plus, average Sunday attendance of between 25 and 30, paid 60% of a stipend – but still closed itself down. Another I know of was reduced to a tiny handful of elderly, despondent people, but somehow turned itself around and is now the strongest, liveliest congregation in its district.

*

In this excellent and inspiring talk, Paul Parker claimed Josiah Wedgwood as a Quaker. Sorry, Paul, but Wedgwood was an active Unitarian who combined a fine artistic temperament with practical skills and a passion for social justice, being a major campaigner against

46

slave trading. The GA Annual Meetings at Keele provided a chance to visit the nearby Wedgwood Museum, currently under threat of closure. The whole collection could be sold to help meet a £135 million deficit inherited from the Wedgwood Pension Plan Trustee Limited, which went into administration in 2009. The campaign to save this fabulously beautiful collection is still very active. (Note: the campaign was, in the end, successful. JM.)

*

Regular readers will know how I delight in learning of ministers who get on the wrong side of the law. The April calendar from Cape Town, South Africa tells of Rev. Victor Carpenter, who recently received the highest award given by the UUA, the Distinguished Service Award. It is presented to only one person annually, though Victor gives much of the credit for his achievements to Cathe, his "Wife, friend, lover, confidante, editor and life companion". In 1962, with son, Tyler, they moved from the US to South Africa to serve our Cape Town church. Nelson Mandela had just been convicted of treason and sent to Robben Island. The Carpenters aligned themselves with freedom seekers, opened the church to integrated worship and brought in study groups on racism. Unbeknownst to Cathe, Victor also worked covertly for the Defence and Aid Fund as a courier, delivering cash to lawyers helping prisoners and their families. He attracted attention from the authorities, was required to report on a weekly basis about his movements and threatened with deportation. The Carpenter family was growing. Daughters Gracia and Melissa were each born with significant special needs. With Victor's effectiveness diminished by increased police scrutiny and the girls needing greater medical care, the family returned to the US in 1967. His less than legal activities continued there, however, and he has more arrests for civil disobedience than he can count.

*

At the Keele meetings I was surprised to learn that the renowned Keir Murren, former Pioneer Preacher and minister of one of the last of the Domestic Missions, in Mill Street, Liverpool, conducted same sex blessing ceremonies. He died in early 1968, so it is probable that he did this covertly, as such relationships were illegal until 1967. Was it therefore an offence to collude with same-sex relationships? I hope so. It would be pleasing to add his name to my 'criminal' roll of honour. I wish I could add my own name, but occasional speeding fines don't count.

*

I undertook a student pastorate at Mill Street Mission and, like Keir Murren, conducted a number of Churching ceremonies, for (probably) single mothers. They were quite legal, and our Unitarian version was called the Thanksgiving After Childbirth. These now seem extraordinarily archaic. At a ministers' gathering one time, I recall Keir, mischievous twinkle in his eye, saying, "I see from the *Inquirer* that the Unitarian Society for Psychical Studies has made George Stanley Whitby an honorary life member. I think that's mean; why only life member?"

June 2012

Happily proven wrong

The ways of churches and church-goers often provide intriguing insights into human nature, especially when it comes to money matters. Many folk seem to think that your religion can be obtained free of charge, and are certainly coy about their level of giving. I enjoy exploring the meaning and subtleties of words, and even found myself enjoying afternoon tea with a sheriff.

A Church of Scotland minister once told me that the most important part of a Sunday service was the offering, or offertory, or collection as the English say. "It's the point where the worshippers make a real commitment to the on-going work of the church," he explained. A similar thought is expressed in the cover notes of the Skinner House publication, *Offerings: Remarks on Passing the Plate* (2004). "The offering is the one place in the worship service where people can make a difference."

This is the only collection of writings I have ever seen about taking the collection, though many ministers have anecdotes to share about what to some is an unseemly chore, intruding on the worship 'gravitas'. Its author, Rev. Bob Thayer, UUA minister in Massachusetts, with whom I undertook a wonderful if brief exchange ministry in 1987, died recently, I'm sad to report. I'm glad I paid him a visit at his home only last November.

*

In one piece in this delightful and thought-provoking book he recalls how he attended a Unitarian church service in England with a friend, and at the appropriate moment produced a twenty pound note to put in the collection. "My friend shook his head at me. I raised my eyebrows at him – why not? He whispered, 'It's a rather large donation.' I felt indignant. Who was my friend to tell me I was giving too much? I flapped the twenty pound note in the air and whispered, 'Are you sure?' 'See the usher?' he asked. 'I know he will be in shock. He may fall down. He has never seen a twenty pound note in a collection except for famine relief in India.'"

Rest in peace, Bob, your book is a generous gift to church-goers everywhere. And whatever happened to exchange ministries?

*

I was pleased to be proved wrong in a prediction I had made about Sir Peter Soulsby, former convenor of the GA Executive Committee. I had guessed he would be too busy now to spare time for the Unitarian movement, but there he was, putting in an appearance at the Annual Meetings in Keele in April. "Last time I saw you, you were with the Queen, on TV," I said, recalling news reports of the royal visit to Leicester where he is now the elected Mayor. "Yes, and she was asking after you!" he quipped. Not many days after, there he was again, profiled in a major article in the *Guardian*, complete with smiling photograph and a CV that lists 'Chair, Leicester Unitarian congregation' as part of his public life, and adds 'narrow-boat enthusiast' among his interests. Alas, it didn't give the name of his boat, or I could watch out for him on the Leeds-Liverpool canal at the bottom of my garden.

Anything else to note? Yes. In November he rejected a report from an independent panel recommending that his salary should be almost doubled.

"It led me immediately to say, in the present climate, it's not acceptable," he maintains. That made me feel pleased to be wrong again, in the unworthy thoughts about politicians that sometimes cross my mind.

*

We often think of the *Guardian* as the Unitarian newspaper, a claim which historically has some validity. Also, it is often way ahead on social justice issues, notably the scandalous phone hacking revelations. We can also resonate with the thought that some *Guardian* readers see themselves as a persecuted minority, or just ignored. Some correspondence described the difficulty people have in getting the paper in some parts of the country. More than one newsagent has said, "We get no call for that one," and one man, in the Chesterfield Royal Hospital shop was told, "We don't get papers like that here, duck." Bad for one's health, one wonders?

*

Meanwhile a hard-hitting drama, showing in Glasgow, about the trials and tribulations of the newspaper publishing industry, is worth a mention because of its title. It is called *Enquirer*, and is described as a shocking new play from the National Theatre of Scotland, and will move to London later this year. If it is as caustic and abrasive as the notices suggest, it is unlikely to give us hints on ways to increase our Unitarian paper's circulation. I'm glad it is spelt differently. I always make a point of writing 'inquire' or 'inquiry' with an 'i'. As far as I can tell, there is no difference between 'inquire' and 'enquire', so I use the 'i' version as a way of getting us some publicity. A bit subtle perhaps, but worth a try. Certainly I don't ever want us to be confused with *The National Enquirer*, the US sensationalist tabloid with an astonishing track-record of sex, violence and salacious editorials, plus some occasionally hilarious headlines: 'Astronaut seen to retain youthfulness as he nears black hole!'

catches the attention all right, and 'Fisherman attacked by giant shrimp' makes me laugh.

I don't think the *Guardian* will ever go in for stuff like that, and neither should we.

*

A St George's Day event saw me taking afternoon tea with the High Sheriff of Greater Manchester and his wife. I was accompanying my wife Celia who has just completed a year as chaplain to the Mayor (a personal friend) of Trafford (where we used to live). I can never use the word 'sheriff' without thinking of the English folk hero Robin Hood, and singing to myself the unforgettable ditty from the 1950s TV series about his 'band of men, riding through the glen', or smiling as I recall the Mel Brooks spoof version, *Robin Hood: Men in Tights*. My tea-time companion High Sheriff, however, was smartly dressed in a militaristic uniform with an array of medals and a shiny dress sword. We chatted about his role, a one-year term which is not merely ceremonial, as is widely believed, but includes representing the monarch, making sure that royal visits go smoothly, and 'oversight' of the judges when they visit the county during legal terms. This includes entertaining them at home. The High Sheriff is strictly non-political and it can be a costly year as it is an unpaid position, not even having an expenses allowance. Why would anyone want to take on such a duty? A high sense of public service, I suppose, plus a generous interest in supporting charities. Makes me wonder what would happen to such posts if the republicans took over. Replaced by a paid bureaucrat, I expect. Well, I shall not be putting my name forward for the job, in the hope of it being 'pricked' for it, a word which dates from the occasion when Queen Victoria, sitting sewing in the garden, poked her needle into the list of candidates to make her choice. Ministers and clergy are not eligible, and anyway, I would feel deeply uneasy in a quasi-military uniform carrying a sword, and even more uneasy in tights.

July 2012

Loos, baths and a stop on Sanitary Street

Further lessons to be learned from what serious matters can be shared in a humorous spirit. And some further moves along the road towards equality for gay and lesbian men and women. Then there are social changes, all in the name of progress, to be witnessed, sometimes with joy, sometimes regret, sometimes pride in our more hygienic world.

In the Diamond Jubilee Concert on TV in June I watched Lenny Henry, a comedian I usually enjoy, though like most of the performers he strained to be on top form on this occasion. He came close to blotting his copybook with his gag to the enormous audience: "All the black people here say *Yeah!*" When a rather feeble response emerged, he replied, "Oh, well, that makes three of us!" Fair comment perhaps, when one surveyed the sea of almost exclusively white faces in the VIP seats. But it was Lenny who was actually chosen to announce the arrival of the queen.

I laughed at a delightful sequence he came out with in a TV show a year or two ago. From memory, it went something like:

"When I was a kid, my mum made me go to church every week; the Pentecostal Church of God of Prophecy. *(Beaming smile)* How's that for a name for a church?

Not like the C of E. What do they give you? *(Glum look)* St Thomas's.

St Thomas's.....*what?*... for heaven's sake! *(Eyes roll, look up to heaven)* St Thomas's Church of the Blessed Radiance of the Epiphany, that'd be more like it!"

Definitely one for churchgoers, especially those who can't see much radiance around the Church of England at the moment. But he got the laugh all right and it's something to think about for those who believe we should change our Unitarian name. How about, the Unitarian Church of the Blessed Glory of the Flaming Chalice?

Lenny would approve.

*

The United Reformed Church is struggling with the gay marriage debate. The June issue of their magazine *Reform* reveals some strong liberal voices, especially in Scotland. David Coleman and Zam Walker, husband and wife ministers at Greenock West URC Church (motto: *If in doubt, try us out*) co-lead a congregation that welcomes all. Their website even advertises a Dinosaur Sunday, but I think that is an activity for the children rather than an invitation to more conservative types. In a lively article they write, "As a married heterosexual couple we are, ourselves, at a loss as to how affirming a same-sex couple would undermine our own marriage," and add, "Some argue that civil partnerships should give sufficient recognition to same-sex couples. But were there not perfectly good seats at the back of the bus for black people when Rosa Parks insisted on sitting at the front?"

*

The word 'museum' still strikes me as meaning a static, rather mournful place, steering our minds to the distant past. Nowadays, attempts are made to make them lively and interactive and the so-called folk museums often exhibit familiar, every-day objects. It's not unusual to hear a visitor say, viewing some domestic item, "Hey, that's not a museum piece – we've got one of those at home, in fact we're still using it!"

Visiting the National Museum of Wales in Cardiff recently I picked up an enthralling little booklet entitled *The Pithead Baths Story*. "It is difficult today to imagine the effect that these had on coalmining communities. They brought improvements to health both to mineworkers and their families, and changed the way these communities were perceived by the world outside the coalfield." In the days when miners walked home filthy to bathe in a tin bath in front of the fire, in order of family seniority, father first, eldest son and so on down to the youngest, there was danger for both the men and the women. Housekeeping meant a constant, strenuous battle against dirt, hauling buckets of coal to heat up gallons of hot water, leading to exhaustion, miscarriages, premature births, rheumatism and accidental burns and scalding. Change came in after a campaign by the Pithead Baths Movement, formed to convince government, the mineowners and even some of the miners themselves that these on-site washrooms were essential. The first baths in Wales came in 1916, paid for by a levy of one (old) penny per ton on the coal. The buildings included medical facilities, a canteen, boot cleaning rooms and toilets. One shudders to think what conditions were like before they were installed, and one can understand why they came to be regarded with such appreciation, even affection. In the 1970s, singer-comedian Max Boyce lamented,

In our little valley,
They've closed the colliery down,
And the pithead baths is a supermarket now.

 Their impact is far from forgotten and in 2007, BBC viewers voted the pithead baths at Big Pit Colliery, Wales's favourite national treasure.

*

On a somewhat similar theme (stay with me) I enjoyed an encounter in July with an acquaintance from the ecumenical scene. Olive is active in the campaign for the ordination of Roman Catholic women. "That's a goal that must seem a long way off," I commented. "No, not nearly as far as people think," she replied. "It is bubbling up in discussion all over the place, far more these days than ever before."

 I admired her optimism and also the pleasure she takes in telling friends the name of the street where she lives. "It was built in the 1890s and was called Sanitary Street, because the dwellings were built as highly hygienic homes for the workers. Later, sensitivities and attitudes changed, so the name was altered, by pruning off the 'S' at the beginning and the 'ry' at the end. I now live in Anita Street, in the Ancoats district of Manchester. And it's now a conservation area," she beamed, proudly.

*

All of this suggests that our present-day concerns about health and safety probably began with well-known Victorian notions about the divine approval of cleanliness, though I prefer Oscar Wilde's version, "Cleanliness is almost as bad as godliness!"

*

There is more. Celia recently returned from a much-enjoyed Unitarian Discovery Holiday at Great Hucklow to report further impressive improvements to the Nightingale Centre. These include increased use of eco-friendly, free-of-charge natural lighting in the communal rooms, which is so effective that it is tricky to turn the lights down, even when you want to. "Also," she said, "a notice declares that with help from the Peak Park Planning Authority all the toilets in the centre have been adapted, so that they are flushed using rainwater."

"Ah, well," I said, "after a rotten summer like this one, no problem there then!"

September 2012

Checking the obits, going back to bed

Newspaper obituaries provide an endless source of mixed information on the lives of both the famous and the less well known. They raise interesting questions as to the nature of fame and notoriety as well as thoughts about how well or for how long the subject and the readers might be remembered. Having penned a few obituaries, I have taken to encouraging people to write their own, otherwise someone else will have to do it, and might tell the truth.

I get up each morning and dust off my wits;
I open the paper, and read the obits.
And if I'm not in there, I know I'm not dead,
So I eat a good breakfast and go back to bed!

I often sing the Pete Seeger version of this ditty to myself and in August a name and picture in the *obits* column of the *Guardian* leapt out at me. Laurence Dopson has died aged 88, and will be remembered by some as, to say the least, a gadfly presence on the Unitarian scene a few years ago. He merited a *Guardian* obituary having cut quite a figure in medical journalism. The writer lists historic churches, local museums, mile posts, seaside piers and steam railways among Laurence's loves, the first of which is presumably what attracted him to our Mary Street Chapel, Taunton. I remember travelling on the (alas, not a steam) train to the GA Annual Meetings in Dundee in 1985, with a good number of other Unitarians who had joined the train at stations along the way. As we were crossing the Scottish border, Laurence's unmistakable voice came over the public address system: "On behalf of British Rail, I would like to welcome on board delegates to the Annual Meetings of the General Assembly of Unitarian and Free Christian Churches, meeting this week in Dundee, wishing you a comfortable journey and successful annual meetings." We all beamed! At Taunton he was for some time responsible for pulpit supplies and persuaded some impressive people to preach, including, I recall, at least one bishop and a senior officer in the Salvation Army. Each Sunday (a good idea, this) he produced a poster for the chapel entrance, naming the preacher for the day. He insisted, however, in adding all their titles, letters before and after their name and significant role in the community. On one Sunday, Eileen Curtain (of blessed memory) one of the Western Union's loyal Unitarian lay preachers came along. There was her name on a poster with, underneath, the single word 'housewife'. So, when the moment came to begin the service, she walked boldly into the chapel with her books and notes under one arm, and, upright in the other hand, a feather duster, which she had found in a cupboard. Not long afterwards, Laurence's patience with Unitarianism ran out, and he left us.

*

In July I spotted a *Guardian* obituary for 95 year-old Derek Legge, whom I had met in the 1980s when, helped by the Hibbert Trust, I signed up for a course in adult education at Manchester University. The obit described him as one of the unsung heroes of the British adult education movement. Though unknown in Unitarian circles, he was well acquainted with the Unitarian contribution to the development of adult education in the 19th century, which was considerable, though now largely forgotten. Who now remembers Unitarian minister Rev. Henry Solly? If you ever spot a CiU (Club and Institute Union) sign outside a working men's club, note that Henry was the founder of such clubs, a significant social service project in its day and this year brings its 150th anniversary. They were not set up as just drinking clubs, as widely suspected. Solly was a teetotaller.

*

Derek Legge taught me that I should not use the old cliché and describe taking this course as going back to school. "One never 'goes back' to education," he said. "That suggests that education belongs in the past, in one's childhood, as though it were an engine at the back of a train, there to push you through the rest of your life. Better to think of education as an engine at the front end, to pull you forward, and in constant need of refuelling. It is not just for children. Learning is a lifelong process. Call it 'continuing professional development'." He had established the university's adult education department. "I had just one room, a part-time secretary and a filing cabinet. First task was to start a library. At one time the University wanted to name this library after me," he said, "but I declined. I'm not interested in that sort of thing." The department has now grown to be the largest of its kind in the country. He was the sort of man one wishes had been a Unitarian.

*

Speaking of those who demur at self-publicity, Tim Berners-Lee's appearance in the Olympic Games opening ceremony caused something of a flutter on American TV. Sir Tim, somewhat unusually, took a bow in the ceremony's historical sequence depicting the transition from the industrial age to the digital era, delivering his message to a (chance of a lifetime) audience measured *in billions*, saying of the worldwide web, "This is for everyone." One NBC TV co-commentator was heard to say, "If you've never heard of him, well, we haven't either." The channel then received a cascade of text messages howling at the commentators' ignorance, many suggesting that it was because Sir Tim is British. Actually, I think it is because he is not a personal publicity-seeker. So it seems the GA's strategy to raise our denominational profile is sometimes in competition with Unitarian modesty and British reserve. Oh dear.

*

Celia and I are basking in the rare experience of getting something right, having read, in the *Guardian*: "Where is the best mix of house prices, council tax, sun, low crime and health? We discover the perfect retirement idyll. The market town of Skipton, North Yorkshire, 'the gateway to the Dales' tops the list of the top ten places to retire, according to research by *Guardian Money* in partnership with credit reference agency *Experian.*" It scored highly on many indicators: low crime, house prices, transport, neighbourliness and access to glorious countryside. *Experian* number-crunched 40 measures that make up 'quality of life' as rated by retirees, with special emphasis on air quality, population density, burglary rates, neighbourliness, good health and life expectancy. Skipton came out top, and they didn't even mention the prize-winning pie shop, or that pensioners get free haircuts at the local further education college. This bull's-eye of a choice on our part is light years away from the achievements of Tim Berners-Lee, but it can go in my *obit*, when the time comes.

September 2012

Of saints, sinners and ice cream

We love our Unitarian history and take delight in celebrating heroes of our past. This also helps us explain who we are, so that inquirers get a better impression and become aware of the significant contribution to social progress many Unitarians have made in the past. But we are happy to acknowledge other heroes and saints too, especially if they have endearing character foibles.

It's been summer of visits, at home and abroad, with some Unitarian-spotting in between some head-scratching about the strange ways of the Church of England. First stop was the cathedral in St Albans. Alban was the first English martyr and his death is remembered annually in June with a major festival pilgrimage and 'Passio', a word defined in the cathedral literature as 'an exploration of the martyrdom through carnival.' The Dean there is Very Reverend Jeffrey John, something of a martyr himself having been the centre of controversy when he was appointed bishop of Reading a few years ago. Some Anglican clergy found this unacceptable as he is an 'out' gay cleric who, they said, had never 'repented' for his sexual orientation. He was obliged to step down. Perhaps someone can tell me why it is acceptable for him to be a Dean of a Cathedral, but not a bishop. Gay and Very Reverend is all right, gay and Right Reverend unacceptable, it seems.

*

At the cathedral he has promoted a display of recently created statues of people that might merit the status of modern saints. It is one of the oddities of the C of E that since Henry VIII separated the church here from Rome, Anglicans have continued to accept the saints that were recognized up to that time, but have neither accepted nor created any new ones. The display prompted me to ponder who Unitarians might nominate for sainthood, if invited. We, of course, are not limited to Christians, but among my suggestions might well be former Archbishop Desmond Tutu. That he managed to pass relatively unharmed through the apartheid years in South Africa I see as one of the miracles required for him to qualify. A minus point, however, might be something he said when he appeared as a castaway on *Desert Island Discs*. For his luxury on the island he asked for a solar-powered ice-cream maker, especially for rum and raisin. Ridiculous! Everybody knows that maple walnut is the only ice cream flavour one could live with forever. Fortunately, his sense of humour under stressful circum-stances easily makes up for this strange choice.

*

Would Charles Dickens count as a Unitarian saint? Following Cliff Reed's bi-centennial appreciation of him in the *Inquirer* last January, my holiday reading has been *Charles Dickens: A Life,* by Claire Tomalin. Strangely, any references to Dickens as a Unitarian are few and skimpy. Indeed, the book contains hardly any mention of his (or anyone else's) churchgoing habits in what was surely a churchgoing era. As Cliff Reed stresses, Dickens's social justice passions were the concerns that make humane hearts rejoice. Claire Tomalin's book, however, focuses less on his religious views, more on his relationships, his vast array of friend-ships, his troubled marriage and what we would now call his worka-holism. This would have been enough to have medics prescribe him tranquilizers, had he been living only a few generations later. He was a human volcano of energy. Also, his dim view of Parliament (his contempt for the 'posh boys', his concern for the 'plebs' - ah, there's nothing new!) made me smile, making this excellent biography a riveting read, highly recommended.

*

Our next visit was to Transylvania, enjoying the sunshine during breaks from a conference organised by the International Council of Unitarians and Universalists, called HUGE (Health of Unitarianism and Growth in Europe). Thirty-one participants from fourteen European countries gathered for an intensive programme of sharing and learning. Contrasts between member groups are enormous, from Finland with one small group meeting in a borrowed room in a Lutheran church, to the Hungarian Unitarian Church, which now covers both Hungary and the Transylvania region of Romania, with its headquarters in Kolozsvár in Romania. Both churches are still in process of regaining some of their very extensive and substantial buildings which had been confiscated (polite word) by the communist regime years ago. In Kolozsvár, one reclaimed building has been opened as a bistro. Try a Unitarian goulash some time and check out their ice cream selection.

*

Telling friends and neighbours we have been to Transylvania usually evokes tired jokes about Bram Stoker's *Dracula*. This year, however, one intriguing response came from two young women we met back in Bradford who told us they had been out there a few years ago, as volunteers in a post-Ceacescu regime orphanage. They touchingly described one of the children as 'feral', *i.e.* badly neglected having lived wild and who communicated only in grunts. This confirmed my view that real human horror stories are worse than anything Bram Stoker dreamed up.

*

Unitarian sainthood is surely appropriate for Francis Dávid, the 16th century Transylvanian Unitarian martyr. On our visit there we went to view the enormous, beautifully restored 1896 painting of him proclaiming the Edict of Torda of 1568, now on public view. Francis Dávid is believed to have said, "We need not think alike to love alike." However, historian Peter Hughes in the UUA World asserts this is a mistake and names Rev. Richard Boeke (in retirement in Horsham but very busy on the interfaith scene) as probably the person who accidentally perpetrated this misattribution.

It is really a saying of Methodist evangelist John Wesley. So, sorry Richard, your own candidature for sainthood looks scuppered. In consolation, I'll buy you an ice-cream some time. Perhaps you'd prefer that. What's your favourite flavour?

October 2012

Photo reminds one of changes in ministry

Unitarian ministry students in 1892. The clothes they wear isn't the only thing that's changed in the intervening years.

Photo courtesy of Manchester College, Oxford.

I just love old photographs like this one. These are the students training for the ministry at Manchester College Oxford in 1892. The effect on me is rather like staring at vintage (or is it veteran?) motor cars and

I am tempted to sigh, "Ah, they don't make 'em like that any more!" I am grateful to Peter Hewis and Susan Killoran of MCO for sending me this superb, meticulously posed picture. The more I look the more I see. The man centre back is sitting on some sort of high stool. Is he the senior student, whilst those on the floor are perhaps in their first year? Smart, carefully groomed, not one of them is smiling and two cannot quite bring themselves to look at the camera. It is probable that the then College Principal, Rev. Dr James Drummond, required that they were all in dark, three-piece suits and white shirts. Many are wearing bow ties and what I've sometimes heard described as 'fling wide the gates' starched collars (which, curiously, my father wore for most of his life, even when working in a factory). All have sturdy black boots, which the streets of Oxford perhaps required in those days. One has a walking stick, unless it is a swagger stick, often carried by men to give them a military bearing, and of a sort carried decades later by 'Young Albert' of the popular comic monologue, telling of the famous occasion of a family visit to Blackpool zoo. This was a stick with a horse's head handle, which he stuck into the ear of Wallace the lion, who proceeded to eat him. But I digress.

*

Perhaps the most notable fashion accessory visible is the moustache, worn by most of them. One even has a beard. This I take as signifying manliness, the point here being, of course, that they are all men, it being some years until the first woman, Gertrude von Petzold came along and caused a flutter.

*

I found myself comparing their appearance with the group of this year's students at Unitarian College Manchester, when I attended the College Governors' Autumn Meeting in October. Not a moustache in sight there, mainly I suppose because the majority of students, four out of five, are women. By contrast, Oxford presently has a three-to-one majority in favour of men. It was notable at the Ministers' September

Conference at Great Hucklow that for the first time in history there was a majority of women present among the ministers, retired ministers and students.

*

Accompanying the MCO picture (but not shown) are their names. First names are indicated by initials only. This was the custom and it was supposed to give some distancing and privacy, a fashion adopted by some poets, such as AE Housman, WH Auden and TS Eliot. Nowadays, for student ministers and poets, first name terms are generally acceptable.

Perhaps the most outstanding student of this MCO crop was S(ydney) H(erbert) Mellone, (second from left, middle row) who went on to have a fine yet almost forgotten career as scholar and writer as well as becoming Principal of Unitarian College 1911–21, during which period he wore a splendid moustache. According to Andrew Hill in *Unitarian to the Core* (the story of Unitarian College, 2004) Mellone somewhat surprisingly left the College in the 1920s to become the last secretary of the British and Foreign Unitarian Association before the 1928 merger with the National Conference to form the General Assembly, a merger which he oversaw. During this era he promoted much Unitarian publicity material, including the widely posed question, 'Are you a Unitarian without knowing it?' which he may even have coined. It is a question by the way, which I find thought-provoking and makes sense until I answer it in the affirmative.

*

It is good to learn that this year there is an increased number of students training for our ministry. I shall refrain from commenting further on their appearance or dress code. A group photo of them would look very different from this Oxford one. I am by no means an expert on fashion and am somewhat conservative myself. In my early days at Unitarian College we students had a small laundry allowance, to ensure we had a clean white shirt for going out preaching which we did every Sunday. I have never worn trainers, blue denim or clothes with writing on, and almost always wear a neck-tie. In my early days as a minister I wore a clerical collar quite a lot, so often in fact that I earned a comment in the GAZette, at the GA annual meetings one year. Some wag asked, "Is it true that John Midgley has had a special pair of pyjamas made so that he can wear his dog-collar in bed?" I resisted the impulse to poke the writer with my swagger stick, but abandoned the clerical collar soon after and, you'll be glad to hear, I wouldn't be seen dead with a moustache.

November 2012

2013

Of poetry with Winnie-the-Pooh, jazz and bible in Harlem and selling the family silver

2013

Of poetry with Winnie-the-Pooh, jazz and bible in Harlem and selling the family silver

What's in a Unitarian Name?

It has become something of an interest, almost an addiction, to watch out for names of Unitarian individuals or places, popping up often unexpectedly. Fortunately, most of these are people and locations that we can be proud of, even if the connection has become faded or even forgotten.

I can look back on 2012 as a good year of Unitarian-spotting, though sometimes my enthusiasm has led me astray. I thoroughly enjoyed a November evening at Rosslyn Hill Chapel, Hampstead celebrating the 150th anniversary of their building. A new jazz composition for choir, organ and orchestra was performed to great effect by Rosslyn Hill Chapel choir plus Channing School Choir, organist Konstantin Gensitskiy and a jazz ensemble. There was also a cello quartet from Channing and a brilliant Schubert solo from concert pianist Sholto Kynoch. The music fairly zinged around the packed chapel to rapturous applause. In the interval I strolled over to the side aisle to take a look at the splendid memorial to the Unitarian Helen Allingham (1848-1926) whose name I had come across in Altrincham, Cheshire when I lived there, as had she as a child. She moved south to pursue a fine career as an artist and was the first woman to be elected to the Royal Society of Artists in Water Colour. I have a biography of her, illustrated with her lovely cottage pictures and there is a Helen Allingham Society devoted to the celebration of her life and work.

*

Then my eye was caught by the name on another memorial nearby. Welby, described as son of the Rev. Charles Wellbeloved (1769–1858), a Unitarian minister of great renown. Welby, son of Wellbeloved? He must have changed his name, snipping the 'loved' bit from the end. Strange, but wait a minute! Welby? Isn't that the name of the Rt Revd the Lord Bishop of Durham, Archbishop of Canterbury elect? Does Justin Welby have Unitarian ancestry, as a descendant of Charles Wellbeloved? Into the computer search engines we must go. Now, what is the origin of the name Welby? Ah, here it is. Something German, 'dweller near a wood'. Not very promising. Let's look at the Archbishop-elect's *Wikipedia* entry. Oh dear. It tells me that his forbears were German Jews who came to this country to escape anti-Semitism. Drat! Not a Wellbeloved then. The thought that the head of the Church of England might have had half-concealed Unitarian blood in his veins had tickled me no end. Alas no, Jewish blood instead. A *Guardian* article described his father as something of a Walter Mitty character with an alcohol problem, who had worked in the US as a bootlegger and concealed a previous marriage. So, Jewish, fantasist, bootlegger, alcoholic or Unitarian? Which would the Archbishop's preference be?

*

A meander round the centre of my old home city of Birmingham yielded better results. The Museum and Art Gallery has a section on the history of the city, in which Unitarians get a positive mention. No surprise really, what with the Chamberlain family at one time 'city fathers', as we used to say, and plenty of other Unitarian worthies eminent there too. In Chamberlain Square stands the Birmingham Conservatoire, a music study and performance centre including a concert hall named after Adrian Boult, he having been an early conductor of the City of Birmingham Symphony Orchestra, some years after Neville Chamberlain had established it. Outside the hall stands a statue of Joseph Priestley, which I was glad to see has not been flogged off by the city council to raise money to pay for government cuts. These are all Unitarian names. Priestley is holding a metal ring in one hand and pestle and mortar in the other, indicating that he is better remembered as a scientist than a Unitarian minister. On the day I saw him, someone had stuck a fizzy drink bottle in his hand, which he is staring at, earnestly. Not entirely inappropriate, I thought, as he was first to make carbonated drinks, though I wish he had been holding a copy of *Errors of the Trinity*.

*

Renowned *Guardian* editor of the past, the Unitarian CP Scott (1846 - 1932) turned up in a Steve Bell cartoon in the paper in December. Now there's fame indeed, though I doubt if Scott would have approved. And how famous do you have to be to get into the *Guardian* birthdays column? That's where I spotted Professor David Williams, who has a considerable reputation in the field of astronomy, in academia and the Royal Astronomical Society, as well as being a very acceptable Unitarian lay preacher. His 2004 Essex Hall Lecture on Joseph Priestley is available on line and he might soon be able to tell us what Mars is made of, and I don't mean the sweetie bar. His wife, former GA President Jane Williams was at the aforementioned Rosslyn Hill Chapel concert, where she shared the news that both of their sons now hold the title 'professor'. Richard is Professor of Contemporary Visual Cultures (does that mean water colours or cartoons?) in Edinburgh and Alan is Professor of Collaborative Composition at Salford (does that include chapel choirs singing jazz?) "Three professors in one family, more than enough for anyone," Jane jested, but proudly.

*

Another name likely to crop up in the news-media is Rev. Chris Hudson, who is heard from time to time on the Radio 4 *Today* programme talking about the resurgence of violence in Belfast, where he is minister. He has a fine track record as a secret negotiator between peacemakers and terrorists.

*

Chris Hudson's Belfast Church is called All Souls, one of three that were given that name. Wolverhampton retains it but Golders Green has quietly discarded it. Too quaint, perhaps? Other Unitarian places of worship have quite charming names. Edinburgh church is St Mark's, our only saint, unless you count St Saviourgate in York. I like the sound of chapels in Park Lane (Ashton on Mersey and Cradley). There is a truly rural-sound to Elder Yard (Chesterfield), Flowergate (Whitby) and Flowery Field (Hyde). The Chapel in Padiham in Lancashire is called Nazareth. Leicester, Coventry and Hinckley each have the Great Meeting. We have a number called Old Meeting House, Kidderminster has a New Meeting and Liverpool has the delightful Ancient Chapel of Toxteth. All of this makes me glad we were spared the name of one church I heard of recently. Rev. Penny Johnson tells me she has just bought the first book of *Old Chapels in the Black Country*, the area of the West Midlands where she at one time was minister to a group of no less than ten congregations. The book mentions Unitarian churches at Netherend and Coseley and there are some interesting old pictures. Two further books in the same series mention our Wolverhampton, West Bromwich, Dudley, Walsall and Stourbridge churches. Among other pictures there is a photograph of Sodom Primitive Methodist Church at Upper Ettingshall. Something in me is deeply sure that Penny is glad that that was not one of hers.

January 2013

Let the Presbyterians claim chapel pub

It is a delight when friends and colleagues from the past, in response to something I have written in the Inquirer, suddenly get in touch, however far we may have drifted in our various directions.

Here's a trivia quiz question: 'Nollick Ghennal as Blein Vie Noa' means 'Merry Christmas and a Happy New Year', but in what language? I was pleased to receive this greeting from a Unitarian correspondent not too far away, and that's a clue.

*

My grandson Billy was sad to miss taking part in the nativity play at his school this last year, having been stricken with the norovirus. He would, were he to meet her, receive a commendation for keeping away from schoolmates so as not to spread the virus, from none other than Rose George, writer on human health. Her book, *The Big Necessity: Adventures in the World of Human Waste*, is all about the unmentionable subject of excrement, our attitude towards it and how well or badly we deal with it. In a recent *Guardian* article she urges us to be more respectful of our microbiological adversaries. Bugs are now universal; they travel both business and economy class. "Health and safety has become a hackneyed joke rather than the two greatest achievements of modern life," she claims, and adds "a fly, they say in Bangladesh, is more dangerous than a thousand tigers." That might make a good sermon illustration, or even a wayside pulpit.

*

Good to see the smiling face of former Unitarian minister Jeremy Goring pop up the *Guardian's* 'Good to Meet You' column in December. This is a weekly slot that introduces us to devotees of the paper who agree to be interviewed. He mentions his unitarian (small 'u') roots as well as his membership of "a relatively new spiritual movement based in Nigeria." This is presumably The Brotherhood of the

Cross and Star, whose followers describe its founder leader Olumba Olumba Obu as being the Sole Spiritual Head of the Universe, and his son, also called Olumba Olumba Obu, is described as King of Kings and Lord of Lords. Jeremy continues as a reader of the *Inquirer*, however, and not long ago had exchanges with Andrew Hill about the origins of the slogan 'Are you a Unitarian without knowing it?' He tells *Guardian* readers, "In the 1960s I sent in so many letters I was asked if I was planning to publish an anthology."

*

I hope Jeremy won't mind if I ponder aloud the thought prompted by a titbit that I remember from the memoirs of the renowned Malcolm Muggeridge (1903-1990), spicy journalist, sometimes acidic satirist and witty TV presenter, later a convert to Roman Catholicism. I met him once when I was a student and was assigned to pick him up at Piccadilly station when he came to speak to the Manchester University Theological Society. I was full of apprehension, knowing that he had no inhibitions about taking sideswipes at Unitarians. I later reviewed some of his books for the *Inquirer* and received a kindly letter of appreciation from him. My recollection is that Muggeridge was musing on the notion that he might have made some sort of career in the world of religion. Had he followed some such path, he would have liked, he said, to have been a monk renowned for his austerities. More likely, however, "some tiresome Unitarian, forever writing letters to the papers." I've told Jeremy that if he ever publishes his anthology of letters, I'll give it a good review.

*

Here's something of a moral dilemma. A colleague drew my attention to a further Unitarian titbit from the *Guardian* which he had spotted. It was in an article by Owen Hatherley, author of *A Guide to the New Ruins of Great Britain*. Headed, From Prayers to Pubs, it includes: "During a visit to Nottingham I had a drink in the Pitcher and Piano – or, as it was previously known, The High Pavement Chapel. The church was opened in 1876 for the use of the United Presbyterians." He describes the building as a "strong, gothic presence" and mentions the stained glass windows of captivating delicacy…"filled with personifications of various virtues (labour, theology, philanthropy etc.)" ….as well as "haunting war memorials." The dilemma is, should I inform Hatherley that he has got the denomination wrong? High Pavement was a Unitarian Chapel. I preached there as a student a time or two and on at least one occasion it was the venue for a GA Anniversary Service. My minister colleague told me he had resisted the impulse to send in a correction, preferring to let the United Presbyterians suffer the embarrassment of having a splendid building lost and transformed into a pub, which, the writer added, "for shock value, is best experienced on a Saturday night." Is this a sin of omission? Perhaps an appropriate penance might be a Saturday night visit there. It could be heart-breaking.

*

Here's another trivia question: What is an incense-override? And did you get the language of the 'Merry Christmas and a Happy New Year' greeting in my previous paragraph? It is in Manx, an ancient Gaelic language which is enjoying something of a revival. It came from Richard Banyard and his wife Margaret in Peel, on the Isle of Man which, I confess, I have never visited. Richard tells me he acts as correspondence secretary for the Manx Unitarian Fellowship so gets all the mailings from our headquarters and takes the *Inquirer*. In the swinging sixties he lived at Unitarian College, then in Daisy Bank Road in Manchester, as a non-theological student. I and other fellow residents reckoned he was undertaking a PhD in 1960s pop music, as he had such an encyclopaedic knowledge of it. There being no active Unitarian congregation on the Isle of Man, he and Margaret attend the local Anglican Church and he tells me that on the recent occasion of the Cathedral's patronal festival (St German), the incense being wafted around the chancel set off the fire alarm in Peel fire station. The congregation emerged to be met in the porch by what looked like 'Pugh, Pugh, Barney McGrew, Cuthbert, Dibble and Grubb' (puppet firemen characters from the much-loved children's TV programme *Trumpton*, remember?) No one had remembered to set the 'incense-override' on the fire alarm system. Might we ever need such a device in any of our churches? Depends how New Age or Pagan the congregation has become, I suppose. It was good to hear from Richard. Perhaps he can teach us to say, 'Are you a Unitarian without knowing it?' in Manx.

February 2013

We are still here, headed for spring

Unitarians are too rationalistic to be impressed by predictions about the end of the world, so do not take them seriously. We can be amused by absurdity, and there is a widespread liking for poetry among us, though I remain uncertain as to how we might react if we were the subject of satirical songs or a show. Perhaps we are too small a movement to be at risk of that.

So, here comes the Spring equinox and we are all still here. On 21 December 2012, there was talk of the world coming to an end, a prediction drawn from the Mesoamerican Long Count Calendar, the one used in ancient times. It calculated the ending of the world on the same day as our 2012 Winter solstice, and some of our so-called New Age groups got quite excited.

At about noon on the appointed day, I was in the checkout queue in my local supermarket. A customer nearby gazed at his trolley full of Christmas fare, grinned and said breezily, "I thought the world was supposed to be coming to an end today; I thought I wouldn't have to bother with all this!"

He got a laugh from folk nearby, so I joined in. "Just shows, you can't rely on anything these days, can you?"

"Nah," said another shopper. "You shouldn't believe all you read in the papers. Anyway, we've about twelve hours to go, yet."

"No," said the first man with mock-serious insistence, "it was supposed to be at five past eleven. It looks like we've missed it."

A woman joined in, though I couldn't quite tell how serious she was. "Ah well," she said, glumly, "I suppose we'll just have to soldier on."

What! The universe has been redeemed from total annihilation, and her best response is, "I suppose we'll just have to soldier on"? Is that extreme pessimism, cynicism, or the belief that life is just for putting up with?

*

If, like me, you can see some absurdity in that conversation, you would also have enjoyed an edition of the Radio 4 programme called *I've Never Seen Star Wars*. Marcus Brigstock interviews guests and gets them to face up to something they've avoided, or just never experienced. (Mine, by the way, is that I've never watched *Coronation Street*. Please don't *ever* ask me to.) A January guest was Rastafarian (i.e. ganja-smoking) poet Benjamin Zephaniah (he of the dreadlocks and Brummie accent, having been born in Handsworth, the 'Jamaican capital of Europe', he calls it). He had never read *Winnie the Pooh* and was being encouraged to look at the stories. That's quite a cultural leap, from the rural West Indian, semi-literate, oral tradition of his parents, via Handsworth to the nice, white middle-class cosiness of AA Milne's Hundred Acre Wood. He described himself as being 'blown away' by Winnie the Pooh, "Because there is so much poetry in it."

"Listen to this bit." he said. "This is Roo: 'I love jumping,' said Roo. 'Let's see who can jump the farthest, you or me.'

'*I* can,' said Tigger: 'But we mustn't stop now or we'll be late.'

'Late for what?' said Roo

'For whatever we want to be in time for,' said Tigger."

Zephaniah was enthralled by this. "Now come on, he's on drugs, ain't he?" he suggested.

There was more:

"Pooh asks Christopher Robin where he is going. Christopher says, 'Nowhere.' So they began to go there. They go there to do nothing."

Winnie the Pooh characters going nowhere, to do nothing, on drugs? I love it! And Zephaniah finds this final piece quite beautiful: "Pooh says, 'Poetry and hums aren't things that you get. They are things that get *you*. And all you can do is go where they can find you.'"

I like that too, and wonder if by 'hums' Pooh really means 'hymns'. And perhaps what he says about them, and poems, is true of worship.

*

In the past the *Inquirer* has published poems, sometimes to great acclaim, sometimes to the annoyance of readers who didn't like to see them there. Former editor Keith Gilley, a poet himself, was keen, and told me that he was never short of poetry contributions, so I suggested that he start a Unitarian poetry society. I felt sure that such a group might arouse a lot of interest and prove as successful as the Unitarian Music Society. This attracts good numbers to its weekends and has many successes to its credit, including CDs of hymn (hum?) tunes. Poetry isn't quite my scene and Keith, alas, is not well enough to organize a poetry society, but somebody might. I can imagine a weekend conference of Unitarian poets, having a great time together at Great Hucklow. No drugs, mind.

*

It's good to get responses to items from previous columns, so I'm grateful to Derek McAuley at Essex Hall for pointing me towards a website of the British Humanist Association which includes the slogan, 'Are you a Humanist without knowing it?' It seems they have stolen our slogan, if not our clothes. Is nothing sacred? Ah, well, we'll just have to soldier on.

*

Also in a previous column, I mentioned the musical show, *The Book of Mormon*, advertised as outrageously funny and a scurrilously offensive satire on Mormonism. A radio interview with Jimmy Osmond added an interesting sidelight. He is the youngest of the singing Osmond family and is still performing, as well as being a go-getting businessman. The Osmonds were 1970s chart-topping pop stars and are well known for being Mormons, so he was asked about the show. "Yes, we're Christians," Jimmy said, adding that his mother was a theologian who taught that there is truth to be found in all religions. I was surprised, never having heard tolerant liberalism from Mormons before. Pressed about the show, he said he had no desire to see it, knowing it was an attack on his faith, but added, "You know, in our church we have a slogan about it. We say, 'You've seen the play, now read the book!'"

*

That's a very good response, making me wonder if any satirists would ever have a go at us. Alas we don't exactly have an equivalent book for anyone to send up. I can't imagine anyone making much of a show out of *Errors of the Trinity*, though perhaps someone with a vivid imagination could produce something based on Cliff Reed's book, and give us *Unitarian, What's That? – the Musical*.

March 2013

Funny Old World in New York

This was not my first visit to New York, but it was a chance to pursue some interests and get a feel for the place and the people. Even in winter the city has an energy that is strangely stimulating. There is a mixture of seriousness, noise, gaudiness, elegance and real beauty. It is also hard work and demanding, best taken in small doses.

"I look like a human tea-cosy!" was my reaction when I tried on a heavily padded anorak, ready for a February visit to New York. Reports of winter storms, with pictures of gigantic snow-ploughs clearing the streets of 'the Big Apple', had propelled me to Yorkshire's outdoor clothing shops. In the event, most days of our visit gave us warm spring-like sunshine and blue skies. The Community Church of New York on Manhattan's 35th Street owns apartments nearby, where we stayed and Celia attended meetings of the Executive Committee of the International Council of Unitarians and Universalists. Meanwhile, I explored 'the city that never sleeps'. Together, however, we managed a visit to the 9/11 Memorial at Ground Zero. We queued at the souvenir shop for a pass, and then through airport-style security and on to the site, still work in progress. The sun shone on the memorial where the Twin Towers formerly stood, two one-acre waterfalls called *Reflecting*

Absence, the walls around them covered with names of the victims. It is powerfully impressive without being sombre. Visitors strolled gently and kept their voices low. An additional memorial is the Survivor Tree, a small, smashed pear tree stump found in the rubble, removed and nursed back to life. It was replanted by Mayor Bloomberg and some survivors, as a symbol of resilience. There are websites with pictures, telling the story.

*

The UN building has recently been refurbished. Airport-style security again, then visitors are reminded that once entering the building they have left the USA and are touring an international zone, with a post office with its own stamps. As someone who was born when the National Socialist party was at its height in Europe, I get very uneasy when I hear the word 'nationalist' in any context. I regard myself as much more of an *internationalist*, so I was glad to learn about the UN building's status. I felt quite at home there, but alas, they wouldn't let me stay.

*

American UUs are very internationally minded. Rev. Eric Cherry is Director of International Resources for the UUA. They also have a permanent UN Office, which has just celebrated its 50th anniversary. It lives in the Churches Centre, on floor 7, 777 United Nations Plaza, and has staff who spend half their days making sure that the Unitarian Universalist voice is heard in UN debates wherever possible, and the other half informing UU congregations about international activities. Think globally, act locally. I like it.

*

Celia buried herself in meetings in overheated rooms, so I decided to Take the A-Train, as the Duke Ellington signature tune has it, to Harlem, the one-time mecca of jazz-lovers. The main street had an amazing array of shops and market stalls in the sunshine, selling all manner of foods and outrageous clothing items. I was offered a suit, 'buy one, get two free', a wig with very long, real human hair, paperbacks that that I wouldn't even want to browse in and glass jars with mysterious-looking, oily, coloured liquids. The stallholder here ran off with a shout when I tried to take his picture. Another sold me a DVD of 19th century women's rights activist Sojourner Truth. "Enjoying the sunshine?" I asked. "I'm grateful for sunshine, for rain, for snow, for whatever the good Lord sends," he beamed. I asked him if he believed the good Lord had sent the meteorite that had caused such devastation in Russia that morning. He said, "We shouldn't question the good Lord's ways." There followed an amiable discussion, with lots of biblical texts in support of our views. "Hey!" I said, "I came to Harlem looking for jazz, and I'm getting bible study!" He told me sadly that the great days of Dizzy Gillespie and Thelonius Monk were long gone, so I strolled off, past a large billboard advertising 'Divorce, $339 plus court fees, spouse signature not needed'. I headed back down into the subway where a very acceptable jazz quintet was busking.

*

Central Park is the lungs of New York City, protected and cherished, even 'No Smoking' signs in the park. I enjoyed lunch outside a café in the sunshine then wandered past the children's playground and the horse and buggy rides to the outdoor ice rink. A 1950s jazz-waltz recording of *Skating in Central Park* by the Modern Jazz Quartet is a favourite of mine. Watching the skaters on this sparkling spring-like day made me understand why it is such a popular pastime here. Every city should have a Central Park.

*

New Yorkers are generally helpful and amiable. One restaurant owner told us proudly that Sir Paul McCartney had been in there the previous week, so he had alerted his chef to prepare something special. "What did Paul order?" we asked. "A fried egg on toast sandwich!" came the reply, "which he didn't quite finish. I offered him a doggie bag, but he just finished it up as he walked off down the street!" Food for an idol, I wondered?

*

Celia's meetings over, we were welcomed at Sunday worship at Community Church. But what's that I hear? Prelude music by Fats Waller! Jazz in church? Only in New York. After lunch we headed for Broadway. Close by the bright lights of Times Square stands the office of the Church of Scientology, where we had seen a non-stop, noisy and sometimes obscene protest demonstration. There are many who have a strong dislike of this 'Church', so we headed for the other end of Broadway to the Strand Bookstore which claims eighteen miles of books on its four floors. I purchased *Going Clear,* an exposé of Scientology not available in the UK. Publishers and bookshops here won't touch it, as Scientologists do not take kindly to criticism. Last stop was the swanky, art-deco Algonquin Hotel for afternoon tea. Dorothy Parker and her acerbic, journalist-critic friends used to dine here at the famous round table. I wondered what they would have made of Scientology. As we headed back to our apartment, a chill seemed to emanate from that seemingly illicit book purchase. Or perhaps it was the wind off the Hudson River that had turned icy cold. Either way, I was glad of my human tea-cosy anorak after all.

March 2013

Struggling with Scientology and 'unpoems'

I am grateful to many friends who have shared with me kind comments about the late Keith Gilley. I have more than once said that Keith and I were very good friends, we *disagreed* about everything! It's only partly true, but looking back we do seem to have spent countless hours arguing, about heaven knows what. One topic about which we had 'meaningful exchanges', was poetry. Keith was a great lover of it and published a number of anthologies of his own verse. I used to tease him saying, "You poets, you twist and turn things, mess about with the language and put us through all sorts of convolutions, with obscure allusions. Why don't you just stop it, and talk properly?" His response was to compose a poem for me each year on my birthday. I have a number of these which I treasure. Even then, I would say, "That's not a poem! It doesn't scan or have rhythm. It doesn't even rhyme. It's an *un*poem!" This delighted him and he congratulated me on coining a new word. During his last months, Keith put together one last short collection of his verses, which his wife Judy illustrated with her own pictures, she having retired from the medical profession and taken up painting. She has had a number of successful exhibitions. I in turn often composed for him a piece of atrocious doggerel. And so our argument continued.

*

I learned that when minister at Golders Green, each year end Keith would deliver a sermon consisting of a review of the books he had read that year. Sounds like a good idea. I'd try it myself but some of my bedtime reading might raise a few eyebrows. In a previous column I mentioned *Going Clear*, an exposé of Scientology I had picked up in New York, it being unavailable in the UK. I can't recommend it, unless you are passionately interested in the subject. Dryden's words in *Absalom and Achitophel* (1681), 'Great wits are sure to madness near allied / And thin partitions do their bounds divide', came to me as I ploughed my weary way through, with my mind soon made up as to which side of the partition the founder of Scientology lay. Much more readable has been AN Wilson's *Adolf Hitler, a short biography*. It revealed a few things about its subject that I didn't know, some of which do not bear repeating. One titbit, however, stopped me in my tracks and I simply do not know what to do with it. Adolf Hitler played the piano, moderately well, and had a good ear.

*

An occasional contributor to the *Inquirer*, Adrian Worsfold is director of music at Hull Unitarian Church. Not a musician but a computer whizz, he finds all the required hymn tunes and appropriate music, carefully manages the hi-fi system and afterwards presents the visiting worship leader with a CD of all that has been played. He is also an artist, and has a phenomenal BlogSpot with dozens of his pictures including caricatures of famous people. He seems to have a particular interest in ministers and clergy, some famous Unitarian faces among them. Recently, *Sky TV* sent Adrian a letter asking if they could make use of one of his pictures in a forthcoming drama series, *The Smoke*. The letter said, "It's about a team at a London fire station. The series will focus on the repercussions for the watch when one member is seriously injured on a call out…" The picture they wanted to use would "be seen in the background in a multi-faith contemplation room in the station." It depicts a pluralist version of the last supper, with world faith symbols in the background and representatives of various world faiths at the table with Jesus, including Don Cupitt of Sea of Faith fame, "though he can represent any man," adds Adrian. The TV series was of particular interest to me. My younger son is a fire fighter in London.

*

Some of our congregations' publications have a title that suggests it is not simply 'the newsletter of' whoever they might be, but that there is more to it. St Mark's, Edinburgh has *Waymark*, a name which I understand is an Old Testament reference, and the content includes longer articles as well as current news. Edmund Kell Unitarian Church, Southampton has *Interchange,* a substantial, occasional publication offering a place for exchanging views. A parish magazine I saw some years ago was called *Spearhead*, which troubled me. I wrote to the vicar who edited it, pointing out that not only did the title have an un-Christian, belligerent sound, but was also the name of the then (but now defunct) newspaper of the National Front. I suggested he change it to *Pruning Hook*, as in the biblical vision of turning swords into ploughshares and spears into pruning hooks, in *Micah* ch. 6. I received no reply. I was reminded of this recently when I read of the Post War Orchestra, a scheme that works to convert weapons, not into farming implements this time but to musical instruments. Pistols into piccolos, Lee Enfield rifles into flutes and a Second World War helmet into a lyre. Percussion instruments are the easiest to re-fashion, but there is now a bazooka-phone. The orchestra has an EP out and performed at a concert in

Glastonbury Abbey (where else?). They have a promotional You Tube video. Creative recycling and peace-making with fun; the late, great entertainer Gerard Hoffnung (1925-1959), who did similar things with garden hosepipes and vacuum cleaners, would have loved it. But I'm sure Adolf would not have wanted to join.

April 2013

Atheists in churches! Beer in chapels!

Pitcher and Piano, Nottingham.

In an era of decline in churchgoing it has been intriguing to watch the emergence of something very close to it, but supported by men and women proclaiming atheism. The fellowship of a congregation, it seems, enjoyed without theology. Yet it is not so long ago that an Anglican bishop had thousands of people buying his provocative little book and discussing it.

The *Guardian* obituary for Keith Gilley did not appear in print but was available online. It included mention of the time that his Golders Green congregation gave hospitality to an American Episcopalian female priest so that she could celebrate communion in Britain, a controversial 'first'. I am sure that GGU's present minister, Feargus O'Connor, would consider doing the same for another controversial character looking for a home, so he may have been tempted by the *Guardian* report that Britain's first atheist church was seeking a new place to meet in north London. It has "been asked to leave the Anglican building it occupied for its ground-breaking services." Alas, Feargus's Hoop Lane church is too small for the atheist Sunday Assembly meetings, which attract up to 500 people. Services have been run in shifts. St Paul's Steiner School church trustees, who have ejected them, say that it's because of the excessive numbers, health and safety and all that. "No it's not," says atheist 'pastor' Sanderson Jones. "It's about moralising Christians. The Sunday Assembly has its first martyr." The closest the church has come to getting Unitarian hospitality will be its new home at South Place Ethical Society which has some past Universalist connections. As to his clash with the Anglicans, did the singing of 'Run Rabbit Run' at Easter make things worse? "Probably," pastor Jones says. As an animal lover, Feargus at Golders Green would perhaps have approved, but don't bother looking. That one is not in any of our hymn books.

*

A letter in the *Inquirer* from Nottingham member Kenneth Robinson, in response to my lament for the loss of the old High Pavement Chapel in Nottingham, now a pub, made me ponder. "The board outside says that it was Unitarian," he reports. Is all publicity good? I loved Kenneth's cry of, "O Ichabod, Ichabod." My Old Testament lexicon tells me this is an expression of profound regret that something sacred is lost forever. A sort of sacredness did fleetingly return to this splendid neo-Gothic edifice, however, during the GA Annual Meetings in April when the Unitarian Bishop, Rev. Ferenc Bálint Benczedi along with his assistant, Rev. Mária Pap, called in for a drink. It often puzzles people to read of a Unitarian Bishop, and to add that he comes from Transylvania raises some eyebrows.

Here's the explanation. Forget Count Dracula, Bram Stoker's fictional creation, unknown to Transylvanians until the tourist industry started to exploit it. The oldest known Unitarian congregations are to be found there. It is now a region of Romania, though the Unitarian community is Hungarian-speaking. Their church is headed by a superintendent minister, but they use the word Bishop, the same as orthodox and catholic Christians. He and Maria also found time for a speedy tour of the city of Nottingham, to fulfill his dream of visiting the region of his boyhood hero, Robin Hood.

They were taken on a tour of the castle, admired the statue of the poet Byron and refreshed themselves at the Pitcher and Piano, formerly our High Pavement Chapel. "I've had a beer in church!" exclaimed the delighted Bishop on his return. Let's hope that the ghost of Robin Hood's hearty henchman Friar Tuck was looking on approvingly. UK tourists go to Transylvania seeking a fictional bloodsucking vampire. These Transylvanian tourists came here seeking a folk hero, symbol of freedom and justice.

*

A few miles from my home, a proper Church of England bishop lies buried in Arncliffe churchyard. John Robinson (1919-1983), was better known as the Bishop of Woolwich. Readers of a certain age may be shocked to learn that it is 50 years since Robinson published his sensational little hand-grenade of a book, *Honest to God*. It was a call for a re-think of our view of God, and was hotly debated throughout the land, on radio, TV and even in the local pub, it was claimed. This was the 1960s era of Beatlemania, the Christine Keeler political scandal, the *Lady Chatterley's Lover* trial and space travel. Stirring times. "Stop considering God as being *out there*," cried this bishop. God could be experienced in a non-supernatural way as 'the ground of being', a concept which I have to say I found hard to grasp. It derives from the teaching of Paul Tillich, one of the swinging sixties new wave 20th century theologians. There is a labyrinth depicting his existentialist theology in the Paul Tillich Park in New Harmony, Indiana. Appropriate, some might say. It was a considerable disappointment to some Unitarians that the radical Bishop Robinson didn't find his way to Unitarianism, as much that he seemed to be proclaiming had been explored by our forebears i in the 19th century, such as not taking the bible literally. But he never came our way, and one wonders why.

*

Far removed from abstract theology but a short step from a labyrinth, perhaps, is the latest project at our much developed Nightingale Centre at Great Hucklow, Derbyshire. Work is progressing on a development featured in the February issue of posh magazine *Derbyshire Life*. It is the creation of a "novel type of meeting room in the grounds. The new gathering space really will be out of this world because it is designed to be an authentic replica of the sort of structure that existed throughout the Peak District in the Iron Age world. The structure will be built from local renewable materials and will have a turf roof." An event advertised in April gave enthusiasts an opportunity to "learn the ancient art of wattle and daub whilst helping to complete the Nightingale Roundhouse. Not only great fun but a brilliant way to keep fit too! Learn how to mix materials and build structures. Other activities include making Iron Age pots and building a kiln." Atheists would love it, I think, as would our Bishop Ferenc. They could happily sing 'Run Rabbit Run' there in the Great Hucklow fields, and the Bishop could combine it with a trip over the hill to nearby Hathersage and visit the (alleged) grave of another of Robin Hood's henchmen, Little John.

June 2013

What colour should Unitarian socks be?

Some fanciful speculations about the appearance of non-conformist churchgoers, some immodest self-promotion and enjoyable viewing of campaigns on important social phenomena, including bees.

Could you spot a Unitarian if you saw one walking down the street? A delightful art exhibition in our local Friends Meeting House prompted this curious thought, initially about Quakers, then by association, Unitarians. A hand-moulded ceramic exhibit depicted a small group of worshippers, seated on simple wooden benches in silent Quaker contemplation. Fluttering above them was a paper mobile of one hundred white doves, one for each year of the Northern Peace Board, currently celebrating its centenary. The doves, like thoughts of peace, seemed to be flying across the room, out of the window into the world. I put a complimentary comment in the visitors' book and then chatted to the artist, along with another woman, both members of the Meeting House.

"I notice you've depicted the Quakers in traditional dress," I said. "Plain clothing, men in large-brimmed hats, women in cotton bonnets..."

"Yes," she said. "That's how they looked a hundred years ago.

"Is there a typical Quaker dress style today?" I asked.

The other woman responded eagerly. "Oh, yes! I often look at someone walking down the street and I say to myself, 'I bet she's a Quaker.'"

"What makes you think that?" I asked.

"Oh, plain clothes, warm and comfortable, probably purchased in a charity shop. And pink socks," she added.

"Pink socks? Really?"

"Well, yes," she explained. "I once joined a Quaker meditation group and discovered that the same people were also in a knitting circle. They all wore knitted socks, and discussed at length how to turn a heel properly. And most of their socks were pink."

I smiled, not entirely convinced, but I do now find myself looking at the socks worn by passers-by, especially in our many charity shops. And I find myself wondering what colour socks Unitarians wear and why. How are the best dressed Unitarians of today attired?

*

"I hope you won't be modest about giving your book a plug in your *Inquirer* column!" said a colleague. I squirmed a little, modesty being only one of my many good qualities. But this particular colleague had helped me enormously with preparing the manuscript and getting it into print. I feel somewhat obliged to take his advice, so here goes. I have been pleased with the kindly reviews of a collection of fifty-two

short sermons, a year's worth, covering the seasons and the main
Christian festivals, that I have published under the title *Wednesday at the
Oasis.* They are from my Cross Street Chapel, Manchester ministry and
the book is selling well at £8.99 or £9 for a signed copy, being immodest enough to think my signature is worth a penny!

*

I am among the many who view with dismay the proposed selling off
of the Royal Mail. There is widespread affection for the friendly local
post office, in country villages, towns and city suburbs too. These mines
of endless information are *ours*, and there is still a sense of loyal public
service, with the arrival at the door of 'Postman Pat', sometimes at the
end of an all-weathers journey. They represent a core of caring and
social cohesion that it would be tragic to see disappear (like the red tele-
phone kiosks), in the cause of profiteering, along with the many beautiful red, sometimes green post-boxes, as well as postage stamps , which
can be viewed in the British Postal Museum and Archive. Who remembers Royal Mail's disastrous attempt at rebranding as *Consignia*? Ugh!
When post offices also became the Welfare State agency for collecting
pensions, social security payments and such like, they became like a secular local church, going there being the only bit of caring, human con-
tact many folk enjoy. A good natter in the Post Office queue can bring
uplift to an otherwise lonely week. We like to take a little pride in the
fact that Rowland Hill (1795–1879) who devised the uniform flat rate
charge system was a Kidderminster Unitarian.

*

My attention was drawn to all this by *Don't Shoot the Messenger: Adventures
in the Post,* the latest play by the Mikron Theatre Company. This amaz-
ingly multi-talented acting and singing group travels the country putting
on plays in village halls and the back rooms of pubs, or even on board
the canal narrow-boat where most of them live. Written by the members and including original songs, they touch on social, environmental
and historical issues, with a dash of humour. Actors take several parts
each and change costumes and sets while you watch. I thoroughly

enjoyed last year's anniversary play about the Luddites, making me vow to never again use that word as an insult. Also, *Losing the Plot* was about preserving allotments. Their recent offering, *Beyond the Veil*, is about bees and beekeeping and their crucial importance to our environment, encouraging us to find ways to attract bees to our gardens. Audiences are provided with the words of the songs, and I felt sure that one of them would be to a well-known Beatles number. Actually it was to a new tune, but try singing this to *Let it Be*:

In the spring (or early summer)
there's a chance that you will see
Sleepy little bumble
Let her bee
Creeping out of hibernation; she won't trouble you and me
Warming in the sunshine
Let her bee

On your toast, or in your porridge,
sweetening your cup of tea
spoon a little honey
From the bee
Spare a thought for all the wonders living in the apiary
Then give thanks to heaven
For the bee.

If the Mikron Theatre's travels bring them near you, don't miss an evening with them. I only wish they would produce a campaigning play on Unitarianism. It would be interesting to see what costumes they wore, especially their socks.

July 2013

Leonardo da Vinci, Mick Jagger and world heritage

Though our religious forbears were puritans, sterner elements of the puritan tradition are not immediately in evidence in and around our congregations. Modest gam

bling and responsible drinking are the norm, though both are treated with care.
Also, most can enjoy popular entertainment as well as fine arts.

When I began my ministry in Altrincham in 1968, I was asked by the Women's League secretary if I minded if they held raffles. "Not at all," was my reply (We didn't use the phrase 'no problem' then.) I've never been much of a gambler. I'll stump up for a raffle ticket now and then and I'm very good at losing on the tombola. The anti-gambling tradition in Unitarianism hasn't been in evidence for a long time but I know of one minister who even now avoids raffle tickets. I've never been to the races, neither horses nor dogs and my visits to betting shops are so infrequent that I always have to be reminded how to place my very modest flutter on the Derby or the Grand National. So it was interesting to read a letter in the *Guardian* from an ex-employee of a betting shop who revealed that punters are carefully watched by experts using algorithmic trading models (whatever they are) and a limit is put on their stakes if they become too successful. Only if they are known to be connected to stables and have inside information are they allowed to win. This is because the bookies are essentially buying that information from them. So my negative instincts about gambling are confirmed. It's a mugs game. Bookies don't gamble.

*

Nor have I ever purchased a National Lottery ticket. I am not disposed to austere puritanism; it is simply that I'm not sure that I want a sudden influx of life-changing money and the problems that would bring. Next year brings the twentieth anniversary of the Lottery, and I figure that if I had spent only £1 per week on a ticket since it started, I would have laid out over a thousand pounds. When I learned from our own Professor David Williams (and I am pretty sure he was serious) that the chances of me getting a large win were worse than the chance of planet earth being struck by a disastrously large meteorite, I felt very smug, and was glad I still had my thousand pounds. If the meteorite strikes I probably won't need much cash anyway. Then again, I suppose I am a beneficiary of those 'good causes' that have been aided by Lottery funding. It's hard to be consistent. I have enough trouble being a beneficiary of the 'gamble' that is the stock market, especially when I think of the problems of our struggling Ministers' Pension Fund and the Widows' Fund that depend on it in these economically stressed times.

*

I've been musing on this since learning of a famous gambler who was a Unitarian. He is best known as the hero of the popular 19th century music hall song, 'The Man who Broke the Bank at Monte Carlo'. There is much mythology associated with this character, but it seems that not only did he exist, but he was an expert, hands-on mechanic who believed that ultimately no mechanism is perfect. By recording the sequence of numbers on a half dozen roulette wheels, he and his accomplices found the one that showed strongest evidence of a bias. Placing bets on this, and despite the efforts of the casino managers to outwit him (no algorithmic trading models in those days) he won a fabulous sum. This did not in fact break the casino, but they were surely glad when he walked away, even though it was with two million francs (then worth about £65,000, the equivalent today of around £3,250,000). He left Monte Carlo in triumph. His name was Joseph Hobson Jagger (1830–1892) and he was an attender at our Pepper Hill Chapel, Shelf. His memorial can be seen in a nearby burial ground, though there are members of the Jagger family with memorials on the Chapel wall. Is Mick connected, I wonder?

*

On a recent holiday in the Loire Valley in France we toured a number of the fabulous châteaux built by the multimillionaire aristocratic landowners of long ago. One that we did not get to visit, in Amboise, is now owned by the equally affluent if less aristocratic multi-millionaire Mick Jagger. The locals appreciate his presence and keep quiet when he is there, to allow him some peace. Now aged 70 he was recently quoted in the *Guardian*: "I am sick of people saying the elderly should fade out and drop dead in their cardigans." Perhaps he was inspired to say this having visited the nearby final home of another renowned

Loire Valley resident. The great Italian artistic genius Leonardo da Vinci (1452–1519) spent the last years of his life in Amboise, in the small château of Clos-Lucé. Somewhat more profoundly (if wordily) he said,

> Learning acquired in youth arrests the evil of old age; and if you understand that old age has wisdom as its food, you will so conduct yourself in youth that your old age will not lack for nourishment.

Tourists can visit his bedroom, the kitchen (he was a vegetarian), his study and much more. There's also a secret entrance used, according to tradition, by King Francois when he wanted to visit the artist discreetly. Leonardo was also a mechanical genius, not for detecting the bias in roulette wheels, but for inventing, ahead of his time, the first aircraft, a parachute, a helicopter, a tank, a ball bearing, a gear box and a cam-shaft as well as a canal system with locks. Many of these have been recreated in the model room along with computer-generated illustrations on videos. The park outside is delightful and though this modest building doesn't match the opulence of the main Loire Valley châteaux, it is much more manageable, especially for older tourists. Some of Leonardo's quotations are on the walls. I particularly liked, "Understanding is the captain and practicalities are the foot-soldiers." A good thought, it seemed to me, for students training for our ministry.

*

The Loire Valley is a UNESCO world heritage site. Odd to think of Mick Jagger as part of the world's cultural heritage, and I can't imagine him in a cardigan. Does his chateau have a secret entrance for any of the royals to pay him a discreet visit? I wouldn't bet on it.

August 2013

Having faith in the street that isn't there.

Coping with modern electronic gadgetry can cause problems, as can finding one's way around our increasingly complex world. Another look at the problems of church maintenance and some memories of everyday street life.

Not long ago my SATNAV went missing. I think it may have been stolen. I had got used to it, even came to love it, especially in our house-hunting days when it proved extremely useful. So I went out and purchased a replacement. I know that many motorists are uneasy about the whole idea, some even suspecting they are operated by the NSA or the CIA or even MI5, but perhaps that's getting a little paranoid. There are countless stories and claims of disastrous mishaps when using SATNAVs. On the outskirts of the town of Todmorden in the heart of West Yorkshire there is a district called, for unaccountable reasons, Portsmouth. A story has it that one day the bewildered Hungarian driver of an enormous articulated wagon got stuck in a narrow side street there, searching for the docks. How do you say, "Wrong Portsmouth, mate," in Hungarian?

My new SATNAV has a nice woman's voice, so we call her Sandra. In truth the voice is clearly computer-generated and, like all computers, her brain struggles with the subtleties of the English language. Then again, so do many human beings. A few miles from my home stands the town of Keighley, pronounced 'Keethley'. Poor Sandra cannot manage that, and confused me with her instruction to "turn right on Kaley Road." Also, Addingham has become 'a-*ding*um'. I can forgive her these, but not the time she instructed me to turn left into a non-existent side road.

*

This near mishap did, however, remind me of a delightful modern folk-song I heard performed by Zoe Mulford a few years ago. She is described as a mid-Atlantic singer-songwriter, spending half of her life in the US where she has Unitarian Universalist connections, and the other half here in the UK where her husband works. She tours folk clubs and festivals and has many CDs and awards to her credit. This particular song claims that devious map-makers have been known to sneak onto a map a street that isn't there. This is to catch out anyone making unauthorised copies of the map and selling them. The song goes on, however, to take a surrealist twist, in which she ends up actually living in the song's title, *The Street That Isn't There.* "You're welcome anytime," she sings, she'll introduce the neighbours, and the kids there play out safely. Perhaps the street is in 'Kaylee', and Sandra the SAT-NAV was trying to help me to find it. I wish I had.

*

Photo: Bill Forray, *Dorchester Reporter*

Had you been driving, or better still walking down Parish Road in Dorchester, Massachusetts this last August, you would have seen an amazing sight outside the First Parish Unitarian Universalist Church. Standing high and lifted up, in what in the US is called a bucket truck, stood the minister, Rev. Arthur Lavoie, offering words of dedication for the beautiful church spire which was being raised up by a giant crane and placed carefully back in its position. This town landmark has been beautifully restored by students of preservation carpentry, and their instructors, from nearby North Bennett School, as part of a long and costly restoration programme for the church. Just below the weather vane on the spire there is a golden ball, into which the minister placed a time capsule.

This work has been paid for partly by the sale of the congregation's communion vessels and other silver items dating back to the 17th and 18th centuries, at Sotheby's in New York, for a breathtaking $1.7 million. I have wondered if any of our congregations would ever dare to do likewise with their 'family silver'. In his words of dedication, Arthur Lavoie said, "We are grateful to our forebears whose silver made this restoration possible. May we always know that this building is only a tool to carry on the mission of the church since 1630, to serve the people of Dorchester."

*

I have a sort of fondness for streets. Four out of the five congregations I served as minister were commonly referred to by the name of the road or street on which they stood, as are many others. There are verses in the Old Testament, in the largely ignored book of *Zechariah*, chapter 8, which describe a vision of a city at peace, with old men and women walking safely in the street, 'each one leaning on their stick, for very age; and the streets of the city shall be full of boys and girls, playing.' And I respond to the line, 'Peace is the high street in a country town', in John Holmes' hymn *The People's Peace*, in *Hymns for Living* 219. This is partly because of the coincidence that 219 is the number of the house where I was born and brought up, and where I and the other local children played in the street. We had a selection of street games: 'Tag' (or was it 'Tig'?), 'Aye-ackey one-two-three', and 'Kick the can', the rules of which I think I can still remember. There were established code words that had their special meaning, such as, 'I've got barley!' which meant I've dropped out of the game and can't be touched. And I can just remember the street party outside our house to celebrate the ending of WW2. Do children play in the street today? I doubt it, as parents are anxious about the traffic, as well as undesirables, attracted unhealthily to children. Were such problems around in my childhood days? Probably, but perhaps we worried less then. Even inside churches these days we are encouraged to have a safeguarding policy in place, for children and other vulnerable folk.

Progress? I wonder.

September 2013

Vive la différence! France is funny too.

Even on holiday the impulse to spot interesting, even curious matters to do with human affairs and religious activities is irresistible.

I've never lived in a Communist country. I've spent short periods in countries that had recently emerged from under Communist domination, and listened to horror stories from fellow Unitarians. They told of deprivations they suffered, as well as the appalling damage to trust, even among family and friends. A recent holiday in La Bastide sur L'Hers in the south of France, however, brought a stay in a small town with a Communist mayor. Former Lay Pastor at Framlingham Unitarian Chapel, Ray Seal and his wife (my niece) Sheila have a holiday home there and described some of the benefits of this Communist regime. Facilities such as the bathing pool and use of the town's function room for your family events are free of charge. The church tower has public address speakers on it, to broadcast news items from the mayor's office, preceded by a 'bing-bong' chime to draw attention. For a moment this reminded me of propaganda broadcasts from Big Brother (the original, George Orwell *1984* nightmare version, not the travesty of it that is the so-called reality TV programme). These French announcements, however, are of little use if you live out of earshot at the other end of the high street, and the one I heard was simply telling that Monsieur Blanc the farmer was in the market place today, selling his home grown vegetables.

*

Sheila and Ray have made some alterations to their house there, including the removal of an unwanted front porch. This revealed that the house had no number on it, so they inquired of a neighbour where they might get one. "Ask at the mayor's office," came the reply which seemed to be the answer to most questions.

The woman at the mayor's office looked bewildered. "You have no number on your house?"

"That's right," said Ray.

"What is the number?"

"Seven."

"A moment." She disappeared backstage and there was the sound of bumping and scuffling. She reappeared with a nice, blue and white, ceramic number 7.

"Thank you," said Ray, and waited for her to produce a bill.

"Oh, no charge," she said.

Monolithic, tyrannical, domination in the People's Republic of Soviet Socialist La Bastide sur L'Hers? I don't think so. More like Trumpton or Clochemerle.

Nearby, next to the *boules* park, stands the town's war memorial, including one woman's name. A *Résistance* fighter I expect. I can't ever recall seeing a woman's name on a war memorial in Britain.

*

Religion in France is puzzling. It is, at one and the same time, a Catholic- country and a secular state. Conflict between the principles of secular statehood and religious freedom has arisen over the ban on the wearing of facial scarves by Muslim girls in state schools. The ban is implemented, though convictions are frequently overturned on appeal. The ban on *full* facial covering anywhere in public, however, is enforced. This might suggest an intolerant attitude towards organised religion, but other things suggest the opposite. La Bastide sur L'Hers has both a Catholic Church and a Protestant Church offering the French version of the Alpha Course. On Sunday the TV channel *France 2* offered us a full morning of *'Emissions Religieuses'*, consisting of: 15 minutes of Buddhist meditation, 30 minutes of Islamic teaching, 15 minutes of Judaism, 30 minutes of Orthodox Christianity, 30 minutes each of 'Protestant Presence' and 'The Day of the Lord', and ended with 1 hour 20 minutes of Catholic mass. No sign of Unitarianism, though I should mention that there is a Paris Unitarian Fellowship. It meets for worship monthly in *La Maison Verte*, a Protestant parish and neighbourhood community center, and consists mainly of ex-patriot Americans. All welcome, I expect, including Muslims and Communists.

*

We observed an oddity as we strolled around another small town square. A symbolic statue of *The Republic* has the traditional inscription, *Liberté, Egalité*... but oh dear, *Fraternité* had been chiselled off. A French feminist protest, perhaps, 'Brotherhood' no longer taken as including women? But what word would do instead? *Communité* perhaps? Or does that sound too much like Communism, or the EC?

*

We also became aware of the grim religious history of this part of the Midi-Pyrenees, widely referred to as Cathar country. The Cathars were a puritan heretical sect that flourished in the 11th, 12th and 13th centuries. Their history is difficult, and complicated by the fact that most of their literature was deliberately destroyed, but there are signs that some of them were at least influenced by Arianism, though not Unitarianism, of course. They regarded Jesus as human, but more specifically an angel in human form. Mainly they were dualists, believing that the earth came into existence not from one divinity but two, the spiritual part being God, the material part, the Devil. They were severely oppressed by the Catholic Church, eventually retreating to mountain fortresses until enticed out then treacherously slaughtered. We climbed up to visit one such retreat, Montségur, perched on a mountaintop with stunning views across the Pyrenees to the Mediterranean in the distance. This period of history is now undergoing revision, with Catholics and others regretting the terrible treatment of these victims of bigotry long ago. One memorial had a bunch of fresh roses laid on it, placed by 'students of Cathar history'. We can't change the past, but we can learn from it and express regret for errors. As for the dualists' belief that the world has both good and evil spiritual dimensions, in my pessimistic moments I sometimes think they have a point.

*

Though retired as a Lay Pastor, Ray Seal conducts services here and there and last year was asked, at short notice, to conduct morning worship at The Octagon Chapel, Norwich. Checking his diary to see if the Sunday in question had any particular interest, he noted that it was the centenary of the creation and marketing of margarine. The opening words of his address prompted great laughter. You've guessed it. "I can't believe it's not..... the one hundredth anniversary of the creation of margarine!" A serious point to be explored about distinguishing the real from the synthetic in religion, wrapped in a little humour. There's a man after my own heart.

October 2013

Female cardinal ? Keep calm and…

The cinema provides opportunity for observations on Roman Catholicism, particularly in relation to matters of family life and relationships. And anniversaries of both WW1 and WW2 events stir memories and raise questions as to how to come to terms with our recent history.

So, Pope Francis is thinking of appointing a woman Cardinal. I was surprised to learn that a Cardinal does not have to be an ordained priest. Some say neither does the Pope, though the embarrassing ancient legend of the woman Pope would probably rule out a layperson, let alone a woman as a possibility for the supreme office for a few centuries yet. I could suggest a few candidates for Cardinal. If she were a Catholic, one would certainly be Dame Judi Dench. She has the stature and the gravitas for it, and the character she plays in her latest film shows the required loyalty.

*

Philomena is an engaging film based on a true story. Dame Judi plays a retired nurse who, as an unmarried teenage convent girl in Ireland, had become pregnant and was consigned to one of the notorious Magdalene laundries. Her slave-labour there was treated as 'penance for her sin', as was the painful childbirth and the torment of having her little boy torn away from her. He was sold (yes, *sold*) to adoptive parents and taken to the US. By chance a world-weary journalist, Martin Sixsmith, portrayed in an understated and authentic performance by Steve Coogan, picks up the 'human interest' story of her fifty years of grieving, and takes her to Washington DC to search for her long-lost infant. They make an odd couple. A cynical ex-Catholic, he is the determined, door-stepping journalist, of a type that, ironically, the real-life Steve Coogan thoroughly disapproves, as the Milly Dowler phone-hacking scandal has revealed. Philomena is tormented by fifty years of painful sorrow for her lost child. The story has twists and turns, heart-rending and delightfully funny moments. But this is not simply Catholic-bashing. Sixsmith has his cynical atheism confirmed.

Philomena remains loyal and forgiving. Astonishingly, glamorous Hollywood film star Jane Russell (1921-2011) gets a mention, but I can't imagine her as a Cardinal.

*

On the day I saw this excellent film, Pope Francis called an Extraordinary General Assembly of the Synod of Bishops in 2014, on the theme 'The Pastoral Challenges of the Family in the Context of Evangelization'. Was this in response to *Philomena*? Hard to say, but it will be a consultation on a range of family issues, including the use of artificial contraceptives, attitudes to unmarried mothers, serving Holy Communion to divorcees, how priests minister to same-sex couples and how churches can respond when gays seek a religious education or Holy Communion for their children. A turning point in history? We'll have to wait.

*

In my boyhood I recall seeing, on little posters in the windows of neighbouring houses, the Catholic Church's slogan 'The family that prays together, stays together.' I wondered about it then, and tried to imagine my parents and my brothers and sisters praying together, some-thing we never did. Nor, I suspect, did any of my friends' families. And I've often wondered how effective that was, as a slogan.

*

Curiously, the war-time slogan KEEP CALM AND CARRY ON has returned to favour. Large red posters in beautiful Gill Sans typeface were originally put out by the Ministry of Information in order to boost morale, a message from King George VI to his people. The poster was never officially released – it was held in reserve for a land invasion that never came. Twenty-first century living seems to have brought the need for a cheering slogan, so this one has been revived. I see it everywhere, often with somewhat scurrilous variations or with additional words, like 'keep calm and have a cup of tea', or 'keep calm and eat chocolate', or even, 'keep calm and get your face painted'. Nowadays, we don't use the term 'slogan', but 'strapline', and we are being encouraged by our Unitarian Visibility Strategy Group to use a newly-created strapline: Nurturing faith - Embracing life - Celebrating difference. I hope no-one makes scurrilous additions to it, unless it's Reading the *Inquirer.*

*

Another film to recommend will surely get Tom Hanks an Oscar nomination. He plays the title role in *Captain Phillips,* in charge of an enormous US cargo ship which is attacked and taken over by modern pirates in the Indian Ocean. These bear no resemblance to the Hollywood costume-drama semi-supernatural *Pirates of the Caribbean,* and there is no grand, sweeping orchestral music. Nor is this a simplistic 'goodies versus baddies' yarn. It even evokes just a little sympathy for the pirates. These real-life, desperate invaders carry guns, and are driven on by violent Somali warlords. It is based on a true incident, and if, like me, you have ever wondered what post-traumatic stress disorder is really like, this film will show you.

*

Distinctly more peaceful news has come my way of a football match organised, of all people, by the Quakers. Called, 'The Spirit of the Christmas Truce of WW1 Relived', the match was scheduled to take place in Bradford's Centenary Square on the day before Remembrance Sunday, followed by an evening of reflections in poetry and music with refreshments. There were no teams playing; anyone could just join in. Quaker football doesn't have winners and losers. Make fun, not war.

*

The WW1 Christmas Truce will be remembered in many places next year. Yes, there was certainly a truce on that first wartime Christmas Day in 1914 (as had happened in some previous wars, including the Crimean). The evidence is very strong that the opposing soldiers heard each other singing carols, shouted greetings to each other and eventually climbed, hesitantly at first, out of their trenches and stumbled into no man's land. They shook hands with their 'enemies', lit each other's cigarettes, swapped tunic buttons and even addresses, and took the opportunity to bury their dead. The best book on the subject is *Christmas Truce* by Malcolm Brown and Shirley Seaton (1994) now also in an ebook. Was there really a football match that Christmas Day? The evidence for that is somewhat weaker. There may be some legend-making here. There have been countless songs, poems, pictures and plays about it, though it may have been little more than a bit of kicking around of a bully beef tin. But the poignant memories of it are inspirational nonetheless, enough for Quakers to play non-competitive soccer in celebration, a hundred years later.

November 2013

2014

Pews, bells and a cigarette case

2014

Pews, bells and a cigarette case

Real and imagined Mandela-spotting

A chance to honour two great men, both of whom died 'full of years' having made enormous contributions in the field of social justice, despite suffering under oppressive regimes, though in different places and in very different ways.

Don't believe your eyes. The camera can lie!

I was unable to resist the impulse to join in the celebration of the life of Nelson Mandela with joy, even fun. Watching people dancing at the news of the great man's death took a little getting used to for 'buttoned-up' British, but that is the African way. The world media was awash with pictures and tributes, and the urge to add my little contribution was too great to hold back. In 2002, Celia and I travelled to Cape Town for the induction of Rev. Gordon Oliver. Enjoying a little tourism we came across a booth offering spurious but irresistible photo-opportunities such as this one, a seeming welcome from the then President to this beautiful city. Yes, it is a complete fake; I didn't really meet him. I can only hope that Madiba, as he was affectionately known, would forgive me. He had a good sense of humour. I love the fact that he often said of himself, "I'm an unemployed pensioner with a criminal record."

I can't even claim that, unless you count a couple of speeding tickets.

*

Gordon Oliver, as Mayor of Cape Town, with Nelson Mandela

A valid claim to have met Mandela can be made by Rev. Gordon Oliver, who, prior to becoming Cape Town's Unitarian Minister had been an anti-apartheid city councillor and eventually Mayor. He acquired his criminal record, at least in theory, when, as Mayor, he took part in a banned anti-apartheid march. At the end of it he addressed the crowd of thousands through a megaphone from the balcony of City Hall, and bestowed upon them all the freedom of the city. Soon after, Nelson Mandela was released from prison and led a triumphant march into Cape Town. Gordon welcomed him to City Hall with a hug and ushered him to that same balcony to make his first public speech as a free man.

*

Unitarian-spotting continued in 2013. In December, BBC TV's *Gardeners' World* visited Beatrix Potter's Lake District cottage garden at Hill Top. Presenter Carol Klein's northern accent described it all as '*woondaful!*' A *Mastermind* contestant had a go at the life of Elizabeth Gaskell, and on *University Challenge* the novelist, war poet and former Lord Mayor of Norwich, R.H. Mottram (1883-1971) got a mention. Protégé and biographer of John Galsworthy, he was President of the GA during World War 2. Also, my bedtime reading of a biography of Michael Foot mentioned Reginald Sorensen (1881-1971), pacifist Labour MP and Unitarian minister who ended up as Baron Sorensen of Leyton. Was he our last Unitarian member of the House of Lords? Not one of the above was described, in what I saw or read, as Unitarian. However, our public profile is getting a boost. As I write, Rev. Jim Corrigall is booked to appear on BBC Radio 4 *Thought for the Day*. This 'first' has come about because Tim Berners-Lee (of World Wide Web fame) is acting as guest editor of the programme. It's on Boxing Day, also known as the Feast of St Stephen who was the first Christian martyr, stoned to death for alleged blasphemy (see *Acts* ch. 7). Let's hope this is not an omen.

*

The year past saw the death aged 97 years of Rev. Ferenc Nagy (pronounced 'nodge', it means 'large'), Unitarian minister of renown in the Transylvania region of Romania. Known as 'Feribaci', 'uncle Feri', he had a life-long ministry which included the appalling privations of the communist era. He did manage to obtain permission to spend some months in the 1970s at Unitarian College Manchester as a Sharpe Hungarian Scholar and valued this and other international contacts enormously. He and his congregation, along with many others, received help and support from British and other far-off Unitarians. Notable among these was our Urmston congregation, who acquired an old ambulance and filled it with supplies of food, clothing and medication. Volunteers drove it to Transylvania where Uncle Feri ran a free-of-charge clinic in his vestry. A small team of local doctors undertook diagnoses and dispensed medication to those unable to afford it, including the despised gypsy community. Frances Teagle of Urmston and others raised money and paid a series of visits following the nightmare Ceausescu years, transporting clothing, coffee, chocolates, toiletries and plastic buckets of pain-killers (there being none available to the general public) as well as family planning aids, some of which were probably illegal; and not forgetting the 'friendly gifts' to keep the border guards looking the other way. More 'illegal' activities to help the oppressed? Mandela would surely have approved. Uncle Feri never forgot this help, and paid a joyful return visit to Urmston some years later.

January 2014

A few alternative thoughts

By a curious turn of circumstance, Unitarians were given a long-awaited opportunity to deliver the Thought for the Day slot on BBC radio. This was on Boxing Day 2013, arising from the fact that Sir Tim Berners-Lee had been invited to act as guest editor for the programme for that day. As a committed Unitarian Universalist in the US, he asked for a Unitarian presenter for the Thought. It has never been clear why it is that the BBC have been reluctant for this to happen. Sure enough, the outcome of their decision was not quite what anyone expected, but no harm done.

When 26 December 2013 arrived I was reminded of the complaint about London buses. "You wait ages for one, and then two come at once!" So it was with Unitarian ministers appearing on the BBC Radio 4 *Today* programme. Having gone for years with, it seemed, no hope of ever having a Unitarian presenter of the *Thought for the Day*, we suddenly get two on the same programme, albeit one of them, Rev. Andy Pakula, describes himself as a Unitarian atheist and offered an *Alternative Thought for the Day*. Some of us are content to be thought of as alternative, and for years we promoted our denomination as 'Outside the Mainstream'. Others dislike it, feeling it consigns us to the margins among groups or even cults that are not to be taken seriously. The 'powers that be' at the BBC may have had thoughts of this kind, hence their reluctance. If they allowed one non-theistic (the word I prefer) presenter, would they be under pressure to allow some less desirable non-theistic groups to have a look in? But allow us they did with a second contribution of a more conventional kind from Rev. Jim Corrigall. As for Andy Pakula's contribution, it was the late Rev. Arthur Long, I recall, who used to say, "Just because God isn't named or even mentioned, doesn't mean (s)he isn't there."

*

Many years ago I participated in a workshop on religious broadcasting held at Unitarian College. The speaker was, curiously, a Dominican monk with an interest in the subject as a sort of sideline. Having taken us through sessions on microphone skills and script preparation, he invited questions. A student asked, "How do we get in? How do we break into the world of broadcasting?"

The monk gave a wry smile. "You offer to do a 'God-slot' on local radio at 8 o'clock on a Sunday morning in August. The only people likely to be listening at that time are *you*, your mother and your auntie, if you tell them you're going to be on. But at least, it will give you a start!"

Not long after that I was invited to broadcast on local radio at 8 o'clock on a Sunday in August, albeit in the evening. I was doubtful about how many people were listening, which leads me to wonder how many people were awake on Boxing Day morning to listen first to Rev. Andy Pakula's 'alternative', and an hour later, Rev. Jim Corrigall's 'thought'. Perhaps it was a low estimate of the listener numbers that enabled the BBC finally to relent and let it happen. Things have moved on, however, and these days anyone who missed a broadcast can usually go on-line and catch up with it. Broadcasts are a little less ephemeral than they were and I have heard of one Unitarian church that had a visitor who came directly as a result of the Boxing Day broadcasts.

*

In a previous column I mentioned one of our ministers who had actually met Nelson Mandela. Since then it has emerged that the aforementioned Jim Corrigall also met him. The film *Mandela: Long Walk to Freedom,* can be highly recommended. I loved and was moved by it. The lead actor looks nothing like the man he portrays but captures Mandela's voice and walk marvellously. I found myself simultaneously disappointed by Winnie Mandela's part in the story yet sympathetic to her appallingly cruel treatment and plight, excellently portrayed. It is an honest, thought-provoking and inspiring film, leaving me wanting to know more, and wishing I had done more during the anti-apartheid boycott of South African goods. Did my passing over of South African grapes, oranges and white wine in the supermarkets make any difference?

*

A study day in December, *The Art of the Jazz Age,* was a marvellous excursion through the world of art deco. Tutor Adrian Sumner is a County Arts Development Officer, so I mentioned to him the windows in our Pepper Hill Chapel, Shelf, and later sent him a picture, though I always find stained glass windows difficult to photograph. The chapel has eight of these superb identical examples of art deco, all in full view from the interior though not from the exterior as they are protected by wire cages. They measure about seven feet high by three feet wide. Adrian's reply told me that he thought the windows "lovely and something of a rarity in church/chapel/ecclesiastical design even in those buildings which are in the art deco style themselves." I know nothing of the provenance of the windows, but they must have been costly in their day.

*

I have a longstanding interest in Unitarian stained glass windows and have a good look at them wherever I go. Some are fabulously valuable, and I'm developing a theory that there is a distinctive style of Unitarian stained glass, indicated by the topics they depict. The parable of the Sower features a lot, as does the Good Samaritan. I know of one that seems to illustrate 'The pen is mightier than the sword' (Edward Bulwer-Lytton) and another, which has children gathered around Jesus, includes a black child. Chesterfield's Anglican Cathedral, remarkably enough, has a window depicting a number of historic buildings in the city, including our nearby Unitarian Chapel. There is a marvellous book to be written about all of this, by someone with far more knowledge and expertise than I have. Also, a study day on art and atheism might be interesting. I wonder what atheists would put in their stained glass windows? There's another alternative thought for the day.

February 2014

Reporting from the Big (frozen) Apple

The International Council of Unitarians and Universalists' major gatherings are always a joy to attend and participate, meeting up with representatives from around the world, including long-standing friends and making new ones from new countries. It is stimulating to learn from our differences, and humbling to find that others learn from us. There was a chance, also, to visit some New York churches.

Hurray! Off to New York for the International Council of Unitarians and Universalists (ICUU) biennial (that's every two years) gathering. My wife Celia is a member of its Executive Committee and helped organise this event plus an additional conference for ministers. Checking weather forecasts, I was relieved to see that they were reporting 10 degrees, only to discover to my astonishment that in the US they work in Fahrenheit, so 10F means 12C below zero! Forearmed, or should I say 'forelegged' with this news, I donned my enormous tea-cosy anorak, woolly hat and scarf plus a more intimate thermal undergarment, the nature of which I'll leave you to guess, though my name gives a clue.

*

The ICUU meetings were held at the Unitarian Universalist Congregation at Shelter Rock, Manhasset, on Long Island. This congregation is renowned for its massive endowment and fabulous premises. An extraordinarily generous bequest of oil well rights some decades ago brings in an annual income figure with so many zeros on it one's head begins to spin. With this the growing congregation has built a beautiful sanctuary plus well-staffed and luxuriously extensive premises set in delightful grounds, big enough to accommodate our conference of over a hundred and twenty people. In addition, more than fifty of their volunteers turned out to shop, prepare, cook, set up, serve and clean up after three lunches and three dinners. They served us in coffee breaks, assisted with the welcome party and pre-dinner reception, guided us to various activity rooms and staffed their information desk and bookshop in the main lobby, adding other tasks as they arose. It was delightfully reassuring to see folk on hand wearing their name tags and 'ask me' placards.

*

We shared Sunday morning worship with the Shelter Rock congregation who were thrilled to learn that there are growing numbers of UUs of many languages, colours, traditions and cultures all around the world. As Executive Secretary Steve Dick put it, "We have members now on every continent except Antarctica, so if anyone has contacts there, be sure to let me know!" Three sermons from ICUU representatives included Celia Midgley who gave a description of her life and experience and reminded everyone that the idea of creating ICUU came from Britain. There was lots of music and singing and sharing and the climax was a surprise visit from the children of the congregation with their brilliantly colourful dragon, which danced its way around the chapel to celebrate the Chinese New Year.

*

Churchgoing in the US is varied and thought-provoking. We transferred to the Community Church of New York in Manhattan for the opening of the Ministers' Conference. The congregation there is grieving for the loss of one of their members, the renowned folk singer-songwriter and activist, Pete Seeger. For almost the whole of his 94 years he sang and marched for peace and justice. Harassed as an (alleged) communist, condemned by a McCarthyite hearing, he reached the peak of his renown leading the singing of *We Shall Overcome* for the 1960s Civil Rights marches, a record of which I have that still gives me shivers down the spine. I saw him once in a small coffee bar in Birmingham when I was a teenager, marvelled at his banjo-picking skills and joined in his songs in support of 'labor unions'. He joined Community Church a few years ago. *UU World* tells us: 'Asked whether any of his many songs is specifically Unitarian Universalist, he mentions 'Old Hundred', which he calls his 'unorthodoxology':

All people that on earth do dwell,
Sing out for peace 'tween heav'n and hell.
'Tween East and West and low and high,
Sing! Peace on earth and sea and sky.

"It hasn't been picked up by a single hymnal," he laughs. "On the other hand, I've never been kicked out of church for singing it.'"

*

All Souls UU Church on Lexington Avenue, also in Manhattan, is an altogether different experience. This enormous, beautiful UU cathedral has large congregations at two morning services per Sunday, a robed choir, a children's choir, two trumpets along with the organ in the gallery and a long list of busy midweek activities. Ironically, the sermon was mainly about the growing concern for the decline in church-going in the US. "Church needs a make-over," Rev. Galen Guengerich proclaimed. "We should start telling the world about the evidence that people involved in religion are healthier, happier and live longer than those who are not." I wondered if that would make a useful strap-line that we could use in the UK.

*

A little free time gave a few of us the chance to see the, gritty, black and white realism film *Nebraska*. Far away from swinging New York City, this wide, largely barren state witnesses much rural poverty. The film tells of an elderly resident who has fallen for a magazine scam telling him he could have won a million dollars. He trudges off to claim his prize, leaving a trail of gossip, sadness and family strife in his wake. The magazine secretary finally tells him he is not a lucky winner, and asks his hapless son, who has accompanied him on this fruitless excursion, "Does your father have Alzheimer's?"

"No. He just believes what people tell him."

"Oh, that's *too* bad."

*

I also enjoyed a tour of Radio City Music Hall, a fabulous 1930s art deco cinema which also hosts shows and musicals. Seating over six thousand it is the largest theatre in the world, with amazing stage facilities and acoustics. Still puzzled why church-going at the local level declines, while ICUU group membership world-wide is growing apace, I briefly wondered if ICUU executive officer Steve Dick might one day book this opulent picture palace for our ICUU gathering, singing to the mighty Wurlitzer. Along with the shows and musicals have always gone live dance routines from the Rockettes. These super-fit women undertake high-kick, Tiller Girl style routines, several times daily. One of them was available for a photo-opportunity so I now have, secreted away, a picture of me with her displaying her fabulous dancer's legs. I was relieved that I was not expected to show mine, with or without the long-johns.

March 2014

Faith you die for: Doctrine you kill for

From time to time it seems important to look at ideas, the theological notions and doctrines that put our faith into words. Unitarians are willing to do that, as long as we have the freedom to revise those ideas from time to time. We do not like to hold anyone to any statements of belief, as in a creed, but are content to take it all to pieces and put it back together again and see what holds true.

Melvyn Bragg's March Radio4 programme *In Our Time*, caught my interest but was a disappointing in-depth discussion of the doctrine of the trinity. The fact that this complex theological concept had constantly divided Christians was noted, but scarce mention of our centuries-old denomination that emerged out of a denial of the doctrine. This is despite the fact that one of the speakers, Martin Palmer, delivered the 1990 Essex Hall Lecture (on conservation), so he knows us. There was also careful avoidance of the fact that for a long time anyone rejecting the trinity, Jews, Muslims or Unitarians risked life and liberty. As Tony Benn liked to put it, "A faith is something you die for, a doctrine is something you kill for. There is all the difference in the world." The suggestion made by Melvyn Bragg, that those who upheld the trinity did so merely to distinguish themselves from those that did not, was brushed away. Discussion of the fine theological details of the doctrine became abstruse, reminding me of the oft-mentioned remark that to be a good Christian one is not supposed to understand the trinity, simply affirm it. In my home town of Skipton we have two churches that bear the name: a plain Trinity Church (Methodist) and a few minutes' walk away, Holy Trinity, the parish church. A friend is an active member at the first but sings in the choir at the second. I must inquire what difference the 'holy' attribution makes. And will the two ever merge? Whatever happened to the ecumenical movement?

*

The late Principal Arthur Long wrote helpful and readable essays on Christian doctrines for the *Inquirer* years ago, published in book form (1963) as *Faith and Understanding*. Alas, a story that Arthur loved to tell about the trinity is not in the book. It describes an imagined encounter between a Unitarian and an orthodox Christian theologian. Out on a country walk together, they are in deep conversation, exploring the Trinitarian idea of God as three in one and simultaneously one in three, when a horse-drawn cart passes them with three men in it. "There you are!" said the Trinitarian, triumphantly. "Three persons in one cart, the perfect illustration, don't you think?"

"No, not at all," replied the Unitarian. "To really convince me, you would now have to show me one person in three carts!"

*

The oneness of God was promoted in the 19th century by James Freeman Clarke's famous five points of Unitarianism: the fatherhood of God; the brotherhood of man; the leadership of Jesus; salvation by character; the progress of mankind, onward and upward forever. These were displayed on the walls of many of our churches for decades, in the US and in the UK, though one suspects that many people here were unaware that they were American in origin. Later an attempt was made to produce new and updated 'five points'. These emerged during WW2 as part of the Unitarian Advance campaign in the US, largely rooted in programmes of modern educational method. They were: Individual freedom of belief; discipleship to advancing truth; the democratic process in human relations; universal brotherhood undivided by nation, race or creed; allegiance to the cause of a united world community. Just why the number five was attractive to compilers of such statements is unclear. The newer five do not have the immediate appeal of the originals, and the so-called iron curtain that appeared across Europe soon after they appeared may have had a discouraging effect on the fifth, though optimists might point to the UN, which Unitarians have largely looked upon favourably. I have enjoyed learning much of this by reading Phillip Hewett's book *Unitarians in Canada* (1978, rev. 1995). It is an enlightening survey of modern Unitarian history from a transatlantic perspective, with eyebrow-raising accounts of UUA annual meetings in the turbulent sixties. It brought me up to date with people and activities in an era that I actually remember. When do current affairs become history?

*

The book also includes Icelandic Unitarianism. It often surprises people to learn that there is such a thing. I had assumed that the faith had spread from Canada to Iceland, only to learn that it was the other way round. During hard times in the late 19th century, large numbers of Icelanders migrated to Canada. They took their Lutheranism with them and those on its liberal wing found that they were nearer to Unitarianism than their own church's orthodoxy. So they formed congregations for Unitarian worship in their own language. At one time there were thirty such groups, but now there are just two. As far as is known, there are no active Unitarian groups in Iceland itself, which seems a pity.

*

Phillip Hewett, now Minister Emeritus of Vancouver Unitarian Church, is an English born minister who has had a distinguished ministerial career, mostly in Canada. He has always been actively involved in both IARF and ICUU and was last seen at the ICUU events in New York in January. It will be no surprise to see him at the IARF Congress in Birmingham this coming May. His other books include *An Unfettered Faith* (1955, see GA website) and more recently *The Unitarian Way* (Toronto 1995, rev. 2015). Widely travelled, he frequently returns to the UK, often taking in a visit to Great Hucklow and can usually been seen striding the Derbyshire hills with delight in his eyes. He likes to quote a titbit in his own book regarding a survey that took place among North American UUs in 1966. One question asked: Would you personally define your own religion as Christian? One minister responded: "I can answer not 'yes' or 'no', but 29 per cent."

I make that less than a third of a trinity. Oh dear.

March 2014

A funny old General Assembly

The task of the Inquirer each year is to report on the Annual Meetings of our denomination. There are accounts of the main business meetings as well as reports of the many smaller events, fringe group meetings and worship services. The Funny Old World column tries to give a more impressionistic report, about the venue and some of the personalities there and the general atmosphere of the meetings.

Whittlebury Hall must be the most unusual venue that the General Assembly has ever used for its annual meetings. It markets itself as a

117

conference centre, training centre, hotel and spa. Close by the delightful country town of Towcester in the Northamptonshire countryside, it
stands at the end of a long drive up to a beautifully situated country
club. The conference facilities are excellent; the rooms, lounge and bar
very comfortable. As we dashed from meeting room to meeting room
we had to get used to seeing other visitors strolling around in their
white towelling dressing gowns on their way to the spa swimming pool.
Some of the meeting rooms were labelled as 'syndicates', which seemed
strangely conspiratorial, and had large, directors' chairs, as well as lots
of hi-tech facilities for projected presentations on screens. It was much
more luxurious than we have been used to, but the long corridors were
all rather anonymous and looked the same. Finding our way around
became a sort of game, with delegates wandering in various directions,
meeting equally confused folk coming towards them, all hoping that
they were heading the right way.

*

I asked one Unitarian participant if she had availed herself of the spa
facilities. "Oh, yes," she replied. "I went swimming early this morning.
Wonderful baths, lots of bubbles and fountains, set amidst a sort of
falling-down Roman temple, with broken pillars and lounge chairs."

My imagination was fired. "Sounds like the sort of place where deca-
dent goings on occurred in Imperial Rome," I suggested.

"Not any more," she replied. "No-one peeled me a grape. But it was
very nice, nonetheless."

*

This contrasts strongly with our previous venues, usually University
campuses, no longer available around Easter, and anyway, somewhat
Spartan and difficult to use. They are designed for a young student population, whereas we require rooms within easy reach, preferably under
one roof, and with manageable facilities for an older generation. So our
headquarters staff have done well to track down this distinctly up-mar-
ket venue, health spa, golf links and all, and get it at an affordable price.
The emphasis on healthy living was discernible in the food. No sign of

any chips, pies, mashed potatoes or pies with gravy; much more like calorie-counted nouvelle cuisine, but with a glass of, er, not carrot juice but fermented grape juice.

*

The contrast is even greater when one recalls that back in the 1950s the annual meetings were almost always held in London, all delegates went there entirely at their own expense and stayed with London District Unitarians. Each year the call would go out to the congregations for offers of home hospitality. I wonder what would happen if we tried to do that today.

*

Good to see Rev. Dr Petr Samojsky at the Annual Meetings this year. Petr is minister at Prague Unitarian Church and has a strong appetite for international contacts. This is his second visit to our meetings, and he paid us a great compliment. When I asked him what prompted him to come again, he said it was to watch and learn more about how we do things. He wants to take some ideas back to Prague, so I asked what interested him. "You are so calm and polite to each other," he said, and added with a grin, "Czech Unitarian meetings are, er, how shall I say, much *livelier*." I think I know what he meant.

*

The centre's Grand Prix Suite is a large exhibition hall where we had an array of display tables presenting the wares of various societies and interest groups, including the *ukunitariantv group*. I popped in late one night to rescue my computer, and found the hall quite empty of people. On the *ukunitariantv* stall however, someone had left a laptop computer running on a loop. It was continuously playing Rev. Celia Cartwright preaching an Easter sermon, to no-one. Early next morning I popped back in to set up my laptop. Again the room was completely devoid of people, and there was Celia on the display table, still preaching the same sermon over and over again. Had it been on all night? I wondered how many times she had preached that sermon.

*

I can report that there were generous helpings of theology in the meetings. One of the best attended 'fringe' meetings saw well over a hundred people crammed into a 'syndicate' to hear Sheena Gabriel and Cliff Reed speak wonderfully about God. A little more surprisingly, perhaps, was the Youth presentation, led by Ian Brennan from an organisation called Stone Soup. The exercise was to find a way of reflecting on the turning point experiences of life, infancy, childhood, teenage years....from the cradle to the grave. In the discussion the question arose, 'What's God got to do with it?' There followed a lively, cheery yet serious discussion of thoughts about God. So if you ever wonder what goes on at Unitarian youth events at Great Hucklow and elsewhere, this might give you a clue.

*

The meetings ended in good spirits, despite having navigated some tricky waters in our *Blue Boat Home*, a new hymn that is rapidly becoming a favourite, even though we wobbled on the last line of the tune, *Hyfrydol*. As we made our way home towards the motorway, I hoped that poor Celia was not still preaching her Easter sermon to that empty room, and that there were no Unitarians left behind, still lost and wandering those anonymous corridors.

April 2014

Celebrating Unitarianism in South Africa

The highway from Cape Town airport heads towards the city with Table Mountain a magnificent backdrop, like the set of a gigantic grand opera. Look left as you travel in, however, and a view of the shacks and smoke of a township gives the first experience of the extreme contrasts this country offers; breath-taking beauty, and, not far away, appalling poverty. These are kept apart by security gates and electric fences for most homes. When the city garbage collectors make their weekly, early-morning tours of the handsome dwellings in the leafy suburbs, their visit is preceded by poor people scavenging among the bins and sacks for anything edible or saleable. Mention South Africa to most people and their first thought is of political stress and strain and division. Quite right, but don't forget this is also a stunningly beautiful land.

*

Minister Emeritus of Cape Town Unitarians and former mayor of this city, Gordon Oliver has worked patiently for twelve years to build the national Unitarian community, which now has six members groups. The main congregation is in the city centre, with fellowships in nearby Somerset West and Fish Hoek. Two more fellowships meet in Durban plus one in Johannesburg, both cities many hundreds of miles away. To assemble representatives for a National Gathering in April was no mean task. The welcome was warm and positive, the intriguing Sufi Temple an excellent venue and with guest speaker Archbishop Desmond Tutu on the programme, who could resist? Celia and I gladly accepted the invitation to visit and join in the Gathering, followed by a short holiday.

*

Gordon likes to remind people of the time that he and Desmond Tutu walked together down Adderley Street. Sure enough, this city-centre boulevard has much to offer, but on the occasion alluded to, in 1989, they were leading a 30,000 strong anti-apartheid demonstration. On the basis of this never-to-be-forgotten collaboration, 'Arch', short for Archbishop, as he is commonly referred to, accepted the invitation to come along to this Unitarian event. Warmly welcomed by Gordon, he beamed, "This reminds me of the time I was in San Francisco to speak, and the woman introducing me said how pleased she was to welcome Archbishop Mandela! I decided this was a case of getting two for the price of one!" That's when we heard the famous giggle.

*

The suggested topic was the role and contribution of religious liberals in the life of South Africa. 'Arch' certainly qualifies as a liberal, radical Anglican, as clearly indicated by one of his books, *God is Not a Christian*. No question that he is one himself, resplendent in his pink cassock and skull cap. His visit coincided with the 20th anniversary of the first free elections after the fall of apartheid, so his mind was clearly full of this. Straying from his prepared text he soon got into his stride, clearly moved as he recalled what he described as the spiritual experience of voting for the first time. "I went to a township to cast my vote, and I can tell you that I went into the polling booth one person, and came out a new, different person. How to describe that? How do you speak of colour to someone who is blind or of sound to someone who is deaf?" (I shall try, at election time, to quote those words to people who become cynical about bothering to vote.) He also believes we are problem-solving creatures, "Though alas, we shy away from the difficult problems and focus on easy ones." Well into familiar territory, he was soon preaching: "God's love embraces all people…. all people, even (and here came the giggle again, and a cheer from the audience) the Unitarians!"

So, an inspiring outpouring from an aging hero of our time, some of it close to the subject, much of it not, but no-one minded. All of it emerged from his generous and courageous heart. Can we claim him as a Unitarian? I don't think so. A heretic? Probably (he quoted Origen, 185-234AD, a highly unorthodox early Christian teacher). A Universalist in the Christian sense? Most certainly, so we can think of him as one of us.

*

Good to hear Rev. Fulgence Ndagijimana of Burundi, guest preacher at the Gathering's Sunday service. He taught me how to pronounce his surname: 'unda-giji-marna'. It all means, appropriately, 'shining under the guidance of God'.

*

Gordon's wife Lizette Robbins, a nursing sister, works for the Ikamva La Bantu Trust in Khayelitsha, described as a 'partially informal township in the City of Cape Town. The name is for New Home. It is reputed to be the largest and fastest growing township in South Africa.' As she took Celia and me on a tour there I struggled with the word 'township' when I saw the extent of it. More like a small city, though no-one is sure of the population size. Half a million? Over 14 square miles of long, long avenues of shacks, with crossroads and side-streets in all directions, with more and more shacks, wrecked cars, open fires burning, some of them cooking whole sheep heads. The Trust has a number of highly effective projects working on health and education, focused mainly on small children with acute dietary problems marring their educational opportunity. A heroic endeavour, tackling the big problems, not the easy ones. 'Arch' would approve.

*

By contrast, the highly recommended Kirstenbosch National Botanical Gardens offer a peaceful, colourful haven of joy. Watch out for the tortoise nibbling the grass, the mongooses raiding the litter bins, then see the Strelitzia reginae 'Mandela's Gold', a variety of bird of paradise flower, named for the beloved late President. Then look up to admire the mountains, a stunning, theatrical backdrop.

May 2014

At the National Gathering of Unitarians in Cape Town.
l - r, Rev. Fulgence Ndagijimana of Burundi, Archbishop Desmond Tutu,
Rev. Roux Malan and Rev. Gordon Oliver.

Photo: Cape Town Unitarians

The people one meets in Oxfam books

Some readers enjoy full-blown book reviews, others skip over them. Here is an attempt to do some reviews without making them too heavyweight or off-putting.

Without doubt the best bookshop in my home town is the Oxfam book shop. Second hand books are cheaper and my favourite section, Biography and Autobiography, rarely fails to offer something interesting. Someone once said, 'The dull autobiography has yet to be written.' I concur, and so far, so good; biographies too. I hope my hearers felt the same about my brief venture into the genre, when I shared a short sketch of my life with ministerial colleagues at a conference at Great Hucklow not long ago. I called my effort, *Bury My Heart in Daisy Bank Road.* Readers of a certain age will understand why. It is the road where our Unitarian College formerly stood, and is for me full of memories of student days and teaching days.

*

I can recommend *Orwell* by Michel Shelden (1991) all about English novelist and essayist, Eric Blair who changed his name to become George Orwell. Commentators are unanimous in praising his lucid prose, awareness of social injustice, opposition to totalitarianism and commitment to democratic socialism, as revealed in his best known novels, *Animal Farm* (1945) and *1984* (1949). After the agonies of a boarding 'prep' school he went to Eton where he edited the school magazine, then served in the Imperial Police in Burma where he witnessed a hanging and became an opponent of the death penalty. He joined the International Brigade to fight fascism in the Spanish Civil War and was wounded. His novels have been enormously influential, notably for the original 'Big Brother is watching you' notion, quoted whenever security surveillance issues arise, as at present. He doesn't seem, however, to have any Unitarian connection. The nearest I can get is that he once wrote a sympathetic essay about the vicar of Bray.

*

I was glad to read *The Old Devil* by Donald McRae (2009) as I have been an admirer of its subject, Clarence Darrow, since reading and re-reading, as a teenager, *Compulsion* by Meyer Levin (1956). The filmed version (1959) of this stars Orson Welles as larger-than-life lawyer Darrow defending two teenage murderers. Described as the 'crime of the century' and 'trial of the century' it is largely a courtroom drama, based on the notorious Loeb and Leopold case from 1920s Chicago. It includes a passionate speech against the death penalty, later issued as an EP record used by anti-death penalty campaigners. Clarence Darrow (1857 - 1938) was also portrayed by Spencer Tracey in *Inherit the Wind (1960)*, depicting the 1926 so called Monkey Trial in which he defended a Tennessee schoolteacher, JT Scopes, for the 'crime' of teaching Darwin's theory of evolution. Also, a biographical film (1991) starring Kevin Spacey was simply called *Darrow*, and Spacey recently returned to the role in a one-man show at the Old Vic. This heroic but controversial character has also attracted screen giant Henry Fonda to the role. Any Unitarian connection? Yes, Clarence's parents were Unitarians; his father was a Unitarian minister, albeit for only a short period. Certainly his social justice and humanitarian passions seem to fit our ethos.

Altogether different is *Said and Done* (2005) the autobiographical writings of Roger McGough, the friendly-voiced presenter of *Poetry Please* on BBC Radio4. McGough was one of the leading members of the Liverpool poets, young writers influenced by so-called Beat poets and the popular music and culture of the 1960s. He has gone on to great things and is now President of the Poetry Society. He came to prominence through the publication of *The Mersey Sound* (1967) an anthology of poetry by three Liverpool poets, McGough, Brian Patten and Adrian Henri. It became one of the bestselling anthologies of all time, revised in 1983 and again in 2007. He has been writing and performing poems ever since. He was also part of pop group *The Scaffold*. Remember *Lily the Pink* and *Thank-u Very Much*? I share with him the experience of childhood amid the bombing raids of war-time Britain, he in Liverpool, I in Birmingham. I do not, however, share his Catholic upbringing or the treatment he received from the Irish Christian Brothers, a teaching order notorious for strict discipline. He describes vividly their use of the strap, not only for misbehaviour but also "as a teaching aid, to get lazy boys to learn a foreign language, or think they were learning a foreign language."

"Let that be a lesson," said one Brother. And it was. A lesson in mindful violence.

*

It didn't entirely put him off religion, however. It seems that the nearest he ever got to liberal religion was this summing up, best read out loud, and with a Liverpool accent, if you can do one:

Here's a tip: every religion offers a set of rules by which to live your life, and if you break the rules, don't worry, your leg won't drop off, nor will you burn in hell for eternity. But if you try to keep to the guidelines, love your neighbour as yourself, you'll stand a good chance of achieving some sort of equilibrium during this life; and in the next, if there is one, you might well be made a prefect and get to wear a badge.

*

So, who's next? I've just started the autobiography of the late Hugo Gryn, Reform rabbi, broadcaster and holocaust survivor. Watch this space.

*

All these three, and the subjects of other 'lives' I have read, are people who have achieved fame and mingled with famous people. This raises interesting questions about fame, or even notoriety, and an interesting dinner table conversation about the most famous person you have ever met?' My problem is that with the exception of Archbishop Desmond Tutu, those famous names that I have met are largely forgotten. Who now remembers Lord Longford or Malcolm Muggeridge?

*

Roger McGough has a delightful poem about all this. Again, this is best read out loud, Scouse accent optional:

> The best thing about being famous
> Is when you walk down the street
> And people turn round to look at you
> And bump into things.

If that ever happens to me, I promise I'll let you know.

June 2014

Pews: a particular type of property

Churches, chapels, churchgoers and their ways are a perpetual source of interest and often amusement.

A delightful story, given to me by a colleague, tells of a Quaker meeting house that went into decline during WW2. The whole town was struggling and the congregation dwindled until there was just one person left. She was of the old-school, still spoke in 'thees' and 'thous', and was determined that that her beloved meeting house was not going to shut. She hung on, took care of the place and every Sunday opened the doors at 10am, all alone. Weeks, months passed, until her prayers were answered. A man came in and sat down for worship. She walked over to him, fixed him with her stern, blue Quaker eyes and said, "Friend, thou occupiest *my* seat!"

———

*

This inspired a sermon which I called How to Sit in Church. There is quite a skill to it, and several problems. Someone else's pew? Sit at the back for easy escape? Down at the front to be sure I can be seen, hear and participate? Next to someone I know? Well away from someone I dislike? The end of a pew, to make it difficult for others to pass me? Many questions. I even found biblical references. (*Mark* 12: 39-41 *et al*). So I was pleased to discover that The Chapels Society, which 'seeks to foster public interest in the architectural and historical importance of all places of worship that might loosely be described as Nonconformist' convened a conference on the subject in 2012, and published papers from it as the first issue of its *Journal*. Fully illustrated, it discusses seating of various kinds and the problems arising from arguments about forms, benches, pews or chairs, and how they should be arranged. Mention is made of a number of Unitarian chapels ('church' is avoided, to stress non-conformity). Our renowned Octagon chapel, Norwich gets a good mention with the pros and cons of its shape, as well as some square meeting houses and rectangular ones with pulpit on the long wall. Should seats face the pulpit, stressing 'the Word' as against the sacraments?

*

Some issues surprised me. I was aware of the old system of pew rents, having seen wall charts with named pews, and numbers on pew ends. I know of a church in 19th century Massachusetts where pew rents were auctioned to the highest bidder, and I once met a woman who inherited a pew rent in an aunt's will. Our Altrincham chapel originally had 'strangers' pews' at the back, for visitors. Rented pews were often occupied, by those who could afford them, at morning services, but all seats became freely available in the evening when the less affluent could attend, thereby avoiding uncomfortable mixing of the social classes. Later, pew rents were abandoned, 'all seats are free' and 'here, let no one be a stranger' notices indicated more democratic attitudes. Even more surprising was the question of whether men and women should sit separately, as they do today in orthodox synagogues, mosques and the Unitarian village congregations in Transylvania. It is probable that segregation of the sexes prevailed in parish churches until the 18th century, and the fact that many of our best loved meeting houses have two doors, suggests it prevailed there too. When did integration occur? It was probably one of those social changes that occurred gradually and without much discussion.

*

Other questions have been about whether seats should have backs, or arms, or be upholstered. Our puritan forbears struggled with this, unsure if places of worship were meant for us to be at ease, and comfortable. With time it became a matter of pride for seats and all fittings to be finely made, crafted, quality furniture.

*

Though democracy dictated that all seats should be on the same level, that the congregation should all face the pulpit and no-one end up behind the preacher, there was doubt about people facing each other. In earlier days the intention was not that people come to see each other, but to be in the presence of God. In time, however, the notion of community togetherness gained supremacy, with the intention that congregants were to be active participants, not a passive audience. The big Methodist central halls, much discussed in the Journal, were built for the working masses, large in number, held together with rows of pews, rounded at the end of galleries. They brought the people together for community, emotional uplift in hymn-singing and powerful preaching. Some had tip-up seats like theatres and at least one dimmed the lighting when the sermon began. One minister reported, "… this was a signal for hands to slip down the side of the seat, feeling for the hand of the girl sitting in the next seat! I think they thought I couldn't see them but I could… But I wasn't worried – I'd rather see them, holding hands in church than cuddling in the back row of some town cinema!"

*

At one time Coventry Unitarian church had tip-up seats. Any others? Should churches reintroduce them? Might it make for a revival? In June, Simon Jenkins in the *Guardian* got me all of a flutter with an enthralling theory that we are entering the post-digital age. Soon, all this talk of apps, streams, firewalls, will be old hat. Live events are in. Glastonbury could sell double its £210 tickets. Concerts, West End theatre, museums, heritage sites, tourist venues, are booming. Arts festivals, courses and debates flourish; poets and writers are becoming performers. Booming too are conferences, seminars, master-classes, retreats and book clubs …"Here it comes!" I thought. "He's going to add, 'and churchgoing'." He didn't, though he came mighty close. He spoke of the growing need for human togetherness, for being with real people. "The post digital means human congregation, and thank goodness for that," he concluded. Was he unconsciously thinking of churchgoing? Shall we soon see youngsters tweeting, 'See you in church?'

I hope so, as long as it is not in *my* seat!

July 2014

Bells peal at Todmorden again

The debate and concern about churches, chapels and churchgoing is continuous. For those men and women actively involved the concern is about whether churches are fulfilling their real purpose. For others, the interest is in them as treasures of art and architecture.

Todmorden Bells restored and ready for dispatch from J Taylor & Co, Loughborough

Photo Courtesy of The John Taylor Bellfoundry Archives

My incurable craving to see a revival of churchgoing was aggravated again on a recent visit to Todmorden Unitarian Church. No longer the home of an active congregation, it is owned by the Historic Chapels Trust as a heritage centre. Recent years have seen excellent work undertaken by the Trust on this large, beautiful, neo-Gothic building and its surroundings. A benefactor left a generous amount of money towards the renovation of the peal of eight bells and a successful campaign to raise the rest of the large amount needed brought us to the sunny July day when the restoration was completed. There are always bell-ringers eager for such an opportunity, so a quarter peal was rung by an invited team at a celebration event. My wife Celia, as a former member of the congregation, contributed to the speeches, a chance to share childhood memories of churchgoing times, when this was a thriving congregation with all manner of busy activities. Climbing the spiral staircase to the bell-tower to watch the strenuous teamwork of the change ringers, we then descended and walked down the long, steep drive into the town to hear the cheerful chimes echoing across the valley. We hoped that the townsfolk enjoyed the merry sounds, and I was careful not to say, "It sounds much better from a distance," as this always gives the wrong impression.

*

I can report that the Church's stained glass windows are characteristically Unitarian. Scenes from the life and teaching of Jesus: the Good Samaritan, the Woman at the Well, Jesus Blessing the Children, the Prodigal Son, Washing the Disciples' Feet, the Widow's Mite, plus a scene I didn't recognise, but the bible reference gave me the clue. *Luke* 10.27 tells of Jesus in discussion with a lawyer, ending with the Two Great Commandments. These windows were intended, we assume, not simply to enhance the beauty of the building but as visual aids to 19th century liberal Christianity.

*

I wonder if anyone can confirm something I was told many years ago. In former times, bell-ringing was encouraged as a valuable activity for village lads, to work off surplus energy, thereby keeping them out of mischief. A disadvantage to this was the problem of having too much of a good thing; not everyone enjoys the sometimes repetitive sound of bells. The sequence 14235 on five bells, for example, is called 'weasels' because it is the refrain to the children's song Pop Goes the Weasel. So the lads were encouraged to take up weightlifting instead, an activity with a similar, energy-absorbing effect, but much quieter. Is this is why their weights are called 'dumbbells'?

*

Todmorden has one of only two peals of bells in the Unitarian movement, the other being at Gorton, Manchester. The United Reformed Church at Port Sunlight has a peal, the similarity of these three places being that they were built by wealthy patrons. Rev. Len Smith has recently undertaken a survey of church bells in nonconformity, to be published soon in *Transactions of the Unitarian Historical Society*. I'm pleased to learn that he has included mention of *Philomel*, a handsome, brass ship's bell that hung in the hallway of Summerville, the former home of Unitarian College, in Daisy Bank Road, Manchester. Generations of students for our ministry were summoned from their beds by its chimes each day, for morning worship before breakfast, and again for dinner in the evening.

*

Missing from the Todmorden event was Christopher Stell, a life-long Baptist, who would surely have turned up. He died full of years, in January 2014. He was a founder of the Chapels Society (1988) and the Historic Chapels Trust (1993) which now has care of both Todmorden Church and Wallasey Memorial Unitarian Church, plus many more of other denominations. The Trust's *Spring Newsletter* has a delightful obituary from Professor Clyde Binfield:

> Christopher Stell had chapel in his bones. Independence, obstinacy, wisdom, humour, shrewdness, pugnacity, pertinacity, determination, achievement, good fellowship, and a way with words, all of them chapel characteristics, were personified in this compactly-built, bowler-hatted or deer-stalkered, bustling man.

I couldn't help but wonder if those 'chapel characteristics' applied to Unitarians too. Obstinacy? Shrewdness? Pugnacity? The HCT obituary continues:

> For so independent a person, he was a serial joiner: the Society of Antiquaries, Royal Archaeological Institute, Ancient Monuments Society, Society for the Protection of Ancient Buildings, Friends of

Dr Williams's Library, Baptist and URC Historical Societies were not half of it. He was assiduous in his attendance at each. Indeed, his presence at an event was a sign that he expected it to be worthwhile.

His monument, Binfield concludes, consists of his four-volume *Inventory of Nonconformist Chapels and Meeting Houses (1986-2002)*. This set of large, sumptuous volumes, beautifully illustrated, has become the standard reference book on nonconformist chapels. It is known among aficionados as 'The Stell' and contains many Unitarian buildings.

*

The *Guardian* also had an obituary for Christopher Stell, mentioning the deerstalker, adding, "for he loved Conan Doyle stories, as only a meticulous detective of buildings would." I have occasionally come across wearers of deer-stalkers at Unitarian events. I associate them with eccentricity, and I'm inclined to add that to the list of endearing chapel characteristics, though I wouldn't wear one myself.

August 2014

That's the Rev. Pedantry to you!

Oh, the joy of exploring words, their meaning and usage, though with the risk of losing friends.

A Saturday in September, a long-held wish fulfilled; I attended a *Guardian* Masterclass. These one-day training courses, led by *Guardian* writers and journalists, are growing in popularity and I chose the one on the essentials of grammar. Having attended one of the old Grammar schools, and received dire warnings about spelling 'grammar' correctly, I have carried a certain amused anxiety about the subject since boyhood. This was reinforced in an early sermon appraisal session in my Unitarian College days, when the late Principal Fred Kenworthy, with a characteristic stroke of the side of his nose, said, "It's 'different *from'* Mr. Midgley, not 'different *to'.*" Writing that, I am aware of the old rule about never ending a sentence with a preposition. Oh, dear.

*

The course was led by David Marsh, editor of the *Guardian Style,* which the *Inquirer* largely follows. It is available both on-line and for purchase from the *Guardian,* as is his other grammar book, *For Who the Bell Tolls.* Both treat the subject thoroughly and with much humour. He and the other presenters were keen to stress that few of the so-called rules of grammar are absolute. Regarding the 'rule' against ending a sentence with a preposition, is there really anything wrong with going to the airport to watch the planes take off? One could hardly say, "off take". He also asked if there is anything incomprehensible in the lament of the little boy, who, at bedtime story time, asked his father, "What did you bring that book that I don't want to be read to from up for?" But I'm not sure of the claim that correctness of grammar is such an obsession at Harvard that even the owls toot, "To-whit, to whom."

*

Another rule that was challenged was 'i' before 'e' except after 'c'. There are so many exceptions to this that it is hardly worth teaching. I found myself creating a sentence to illustrate this, and came up with, 'Neither Keith nor his eight heirs weigh their freight.' It seems, too, that there are instances where it is not a crime to split an infinitive, so it is not absolutely wrong for star-trekkers "to boldly go" after all.

*

Lynne Truss's enormously popular book, *Eats, Shoots & Leaves: The Zero Tolerance Approach to Punctuation,* is a must for those who want to explore the subject and risk, as I did, some squirms of embarrassment. She bewails the decline in correct use of punctuation, focusing on the so-called greengrocer's apostrophe. Why poor greengrocers are singled out for the error is not clear, but it remains common for shops to be selling 'pea's', parsnip's and 'potato's'. (Alliteration: *tick.*) I wince when I see such things, and I vowed that I would never avail myself of the services of a solicitor near my home who advertised, 'No win, no fee's'. Soon after spotting this I was not surprised to notice that the culprit's premises had closed down. Is it so very important? There are some delightful howlers to sustain the humour level. For a woman to say, "Those are my husbands" would suggest polyandry until the apostrophe is inserted, to make it clear that she was pointing to his hats. Worst of all, "Let's eat grandma" sounds like an invitation to a cannibals' luncheon, until a comma inserted after 'eat' clarifies it as an invitation to grandma to take her seat at the table. Incidentally, I once read of a somewhat snooty character who said, "I would be extremely reluctant to accept an invitation to lunch, but would accept with great pleasure an invitation to a luncheon." How times change.

The Greengrocer's Apostrophe

Photo: John Midgley

*

David Marsh shared with the Masterclass students the news that some years ago he wrote an 18,000 word dissertation on the word 'myself'. Hard to believe until one realises how often it is misused, as in 'Myself and my wife are *Inquirer* readers.' Ouch. What's wrong with 'I' or, where appropriate, 'me'? Some claim that HM the Queen spoiled it all with her much derided use of 'My husband and I'. Marsh concluded that people are reluctant to use 'I' and 'me' out of shyness, feeling that 'myself' helps avoid sounding egotistic. Ironically, the opposite is true, as the best use of the word 'myself' is for emphasis. Incidentally, we were told that inverted commas should never be used for "emphasis".

*

Further sessions came from Mark Forsyth and his book *The Elements of Eloquence: How to Turn the Perfect English Phrase.* This introduced us to terms like 'polyptoton' and 'epizeuxis', words so amazing I can hardly bring myself to find out what they mean. Next came Harry Ritchie (*English for the Natives*, 2013) and his thoughts on the order of adjectives in a sentence. So, we say that a lady in a little black dress got on a big red London bus. We would never say, 'A lady in a black little dress got on a red London big bus.' Try it with a long sentence. 'A beautiful, large, old, round, black, Japanese, metal, baking tray.' Now reverse the order of the adjectives. Tricky. Why? And by the way, Fred Kenworthy also taught me that 'reverend' is not a noun but an adjective.

*

Some find this all very irritating and become exasperated at what seems to be nit-picking, as in the caption from a cartoon, with one speaker exclaiming, "Thank you, *Professor Pedantic!*" and the reply, "It's Professor *Pedantry*, actually."

Now, to proof-check this page, again, for errors...

September 2014

Funny old Christmas list: toilet and jazz

A glimpse of an endeavour to bring progress for women in the Roman Catholic church, some flexibility from a high church Anglican and a very down-to-earth way of helping bring community development in the third world.

I really thought this was a mistake. A surprise bulletin from South Africa correspondent Gordon Oliver:

"Last weekend I participated in the ordination of a South African woman as a Catholic priest."

I knew that a recent gathering of Roman Catholic bishops had discussed all manner of controversial issues, but I certainly didn't think they had rushed through acceptance of the ordination of women. Gordon continues, "Of course the local hierarchy of the RC Church huffs and puffs quietly about this. It's a growing international movement, known simply as Roman Catholic Women Priests. The officiating bishop at this ordination is also a woman, a former Dominican nun who lectured at the Catholic Seminary in Pretoria, SA for many years. Her brother is a member of the Cape Town Unitarian Church. At his suggestion, some years ago, I invited her to address a Sunday morning service in our church."

Now it makes sense. Gordon is no stranger to controversial territories. The movement's website tells it all:

> Roman Catholic Women Priests is a renewal movement within the Church that began in Germany with the ordination of seven women on the Danube River in 2002. In 2003, two of the original Danube 7 were ordained bishops… Women bishops, ordained in Apostolic Succession, continue to carry out the work of ordaining women in the Roman Catholic Church... Currently there are over 145 ordained Roman Catholic women worldwide who are reclaiming their ancient spiritual heritage and are re-shaping a more inclusive, Christ-centred Church for the 21st century. We advocate a new model of priestly ministry, united with the people with whom we serve. We are rooted in a response to Jesus who called women and men to be disciples and equals, living the Gospel.

Their campaign song is 'We are Standing on the Shoulders of Giants'. The accompanying video depicts heroic freedom-fighters of the past, including Martin Luther King, Nelson Mandela, Rosa Parks, Sojourner Truth and yes, at least one Unitarian, Susan B Anthony. All those presently involved in this movement are, of course, excommunicated *latae sententiae* (automatically). Sounds like a lively minority movement getting on with doing what they want, and what they believe is right, waiting for orthodoxy to catch up. It has a familiar ring to it.

*

Strange, how names keep popping up. Turning the pages of the *Inquirer* for 13 September I enjoyed reading Matthew Smith's report of the June 2014 Annual Meetings of the Ministerial Old Students Association, at Harris Manchester College, Oxford. A guest speaker at this event was the Rev. Dr Martyn Percy, at that time Principal of Ripon College, Cuddeston. In his address he encouraged Unitarians not to be anxious about their small numbers, and spoke positively about the validity of the liberal religious voice that Unitarianism offers. His name jumped out at me again a few weeks later whilst listening to BBC Radio3, at what for me is the sacred hour of 5pm on Saturday. The programme is *Jazz Record Requests*, and on 4 October a request by the Very Rev. Dr Percy was played. He dedicated it to his former colleagues at Ripon College, and also to his new friends at Christ's College, Oxford, where he has just been appointed Dean. This was aired on the very day and hour of his installation to this post. His choice of record was 'Resolution' from the album *A Love Supreme*, by John Coltrane, which, he pointed out is reckoned to be a homage to the poetic preaching that Coltrane grew up with. "And I'll be preaching while this programme is being broadcast," the new Dean added.

*

So, we have the Dean of an Anglican Oxford College who is not averse to mingling with Unitarians, whose wife is also ordained (no fear of her being excommunicated!); she serves as Chaplain at Trinity College Oxford. He has a long list of theological books and achievements to his credit and has served on various public bodies, including the Advertising Standards Authority. His latest book is *The Thirty-Nine New Articles: An Anglican Landscape of Faith* (2013).

*

And he obviously enjoys jazz at 'the sacred hour'. His choice of John Coltrane might make some readers and listeners wince a little. When I mention jazz, the usual response is, "Well I like some jazz, but I can't stand this modern, doodly-oodly stuff. I like to recognise the tune." Coltrane falls into that troublesome category; definitely 'doodly-oodly', not easily accessible to inexperienced ears, and not obviously melodious. Then again, some people think academic theology is rather like that.

*

From the gleaming spires of High-Church Oxford – to life's down-to-earth basics. In the toilet of our local Friends Meeting House hangs a small picture of a latrine with a corrugated iron roof. This Quaker toilet is twinned with the latrine in a third world country. The website *toilettwinning.org* has the persuasive information:

> Toilet Twinning is raising funds to enable people living in poor communities to have clean water, a decent toilet, and to learn about hygiene – a vital combination that prevents the spread of disease, reduces the number of deaths among children, and brings hope for the future. For a £60 donation, you can twin your toilet at home, work, school or church with a latrine in Africa or Asia.

A toilet-twinning would make a delightful and unusual Christmas present, in the form of a framed picture of a sponsored third world latrine. If I gave something like that I might be considered eccentric, but then, I also enjoy jazz.

October 2014

A cigarette case and a mystery

The 100th anniversary of the outbreak of WW1 brought much reflection.

It surprises people when I tell them that my father was a soldier in the
First World War. Unlike many millions of others, he lived to tell the tale.
He came home and settled down to raise a family of six children, in fact
seven children, but child number six died in infancy and I came along
to replace him. My father was into his forties when I was born, and
when I was a boy he sometimes used to talk about his wartime experiences, beginning with the words, "When I was in the trenches..."   To
me it was all rather mysterious and far away. He had been just an ordinary soldier - 'Tommy Atkins' was the term sometimes used - though I
learned that he had been trained to use a machine gun. I once asked him
if he had ever killed anybody, but he avoided a clear answer by saying
that in the circumstances of battle it was impossible to tell.

*

It vexes me now that I didn't ask him a lot more about his soldiering
experience, and didn't write any of it down. I can recall a few of his stories, and learned more by talking to my older siblings, but I didn't
explore his history with him in a systematic way. I think this was
because I had the strong impression that for him it was all in the past.
There was no boasting, nor anything heroic about it, and he apparently only twice attended a reunion event, one of them a year after he had
come home. He didn't enjoy it and never went again until, I think, 1978
when Birmingham City Council laid on a 60th anniversary reception for
WW1 veterans and my sister had to cajole him into attending. All that
he had ever wanted to do was get away from the trenches, get home and
raise a family, which he did, though not without a struggle. Through the
nineteen-twenties and thirties, then World War 2, life was far from easy
for an ordinary, working-class Brummie family.

*

For many years he suffered from nightmares, and I can recall once or twice hearing him shouting out in the middle of the night. But it was something that was joked about. My mother would describe how she would thump my father until he woke up out of the nightmare, so that he would be quiet, and she and everyone could get back to sleep.

He told us that he was dreaming about a struggle with a black knight; the black of night in the nightmare trenches perhaps?

During the war he had been wounded, twice, sent back for hospital treatment twice and returned to the trenches twice. Up in his bedroom was a box containing some souvenirs of his army days, and among them was a cigarette case with a bullet hole through it. This had been in the top pocket of his soldier's tunic when he was hit by one of a hail of bullets. Again, I never questioned him closely about this, but I used to boast to my school friends about my Dad and the cigarette case which my mother had sent him, filled with cigarettes, as a birthday present, which was in his top pocket and had saved his life when he was shot.

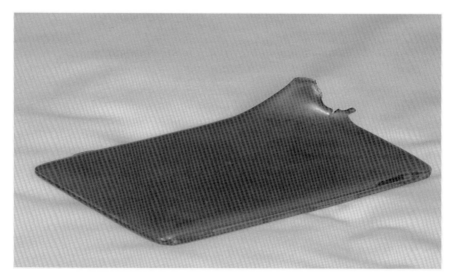

WW1 Cigarette Case

Photo: John Midgley

*

Many years later, as an adult, I mentioned to my father how I used to boast in this way, and I was astonished when he replied, "That's nonsense. The bullet went the other way." I was bewildered. If the bullet had come through his back and right through his body and out at the front, how on earth had he survived? He explained. The bullet had entered the back of his upper arm, gone right through his arm and had caught the corner of the cigarette case as it passed right through.

*

Though it had not saved his life in the way I had imagined, it nonetheless seems to me something of a miracle. If the bullet had gone only an inch or two to one side, it would surely have killed him, and I would not be sitting here at my desk, writing this piece for the *Inquirer*, now. "No great loss!" I hear you cry - and I agree, but something in me is profoundly glad it didn't happen that way.

*

It has certainly made me think. If he had died, there would have been no marriage, no children, no grandchildren nor great grandchildren. All of these would be missing from the drama of human life that has brought me to where I am, writing this piece, right now.

If all of this was missing, what would be happening? Would someone else be here? Would none of us be here? Would I, perhaps, have come into existence some other way - by some other parents, some other time, some other place? I find that the more I try to think that through, the more bewildered I get. I have no answers to these questions. I simply have to accept all this as part of the fragile mystery of existence, a mystery we all live with, but brought home to me dramatically and vividly by a cigarette case with a bullet hole through it.

November 2014

When Berlin's wall tumbled down

A cluster of anniversaries gives the opportunity for a look back at significant moments in modern times. How quickly things change, and what seems to be contemporary news soon turns into history, as turning the pages of back numbers of newspapers and magazines will soon demonstrate.

German Chancellor Angela Merkel symbolically placed flowers in a slit in what remains of the Berlin wall. This was Remembrance Sunday 2014, also the anniversary of the fall of the wall, and it sent my memory spinning back to those dramatic events, 25 years ago. This divided city, the Berlin air-lift and all that the cold war meant, had been part of my life since boyhood. I had smiled when I learned the *inaccurate* urban legend that President Jack Kennedy's famous (1963) declaration, "*Ich bin ein Berliner*", could easily have been taken to mean, 'I am a jam doughnut.' I had shuddered at Richard Burton's gritty performance in *The Spy Who Came in from the Cold* (1965), the only John le Carré cold war story I have been able to comprehend. Now, the wall had finally yielded and was attacked and danced on by joyous Berliners of both east and west. At that time, my son Nick was a student in France. This was a moment in history too good to miss, so he and some friends organised two busloads to make the long excursion to see it. He wrote me a letter about it, which I easily converted into an article for the *Inquirer*. A hoarder of back issues, I find the piece holds up very well. It conveys the strange sensation of wandering around East Berlin, his feelings of anger and incomprehension, the poorly stocked shops, the anonymous apartment blocks, many of them unfinished. "One West Berliner, in a state of near frenzy, induced by alcohol perhaps, had stolen a pneumatic drill from a nearby building site, had succeeded in getting it going and was desperately hacking pieces from the wall. It represents a harsh indictment of humankind which West Berliners want to see brought down, and seem willing to undertake this themselves if necessary. At one point, a piece of graffiti read, 'Au revoir, monument to insanity.' It seemed to sum everything up."

*

Another story tells that when jazz pianist Dave Brubeck toured Europe in the cold war days of 1958, and played to a packed concert in Berlin, he was smuggled in the boot of a car through the Brandenburg Gate, across East Germany to play for eager fans in communist Poland. In fact he was offered this illicit journey but wisely declined. After Brubeck had waited many hours, alone in a dingy police station, an officer appeared with official travel documents for 'Mr Kulu'. "No," replied Dave, "the name is Brubeck." The official produced a Polish newspaper with a picture of Dave under the heading, 'Mr Kulu', meaning, 'Mr Cool' as in 'cool jazz'. Smiles all round and the Polish concert went ahead.

*

As a young Unitarian I enjoyed participating in an Anglo-German camp in Offenbach-am-Main in 1956. We visited the newly rebuilt liberal Christian church there and socialised, talked, sang and danced with the offspring of what, only a decade or so before, had been our WW2 enemies. Some fleeting, teenage holiday romances even flowered. We met the church's venerable, grey-haired minister Max Gehrman, who, with tears flowing as we left, broke a branch from a nearby shrub and waved us off. This experience gave me my taste for international Unitarian youth contacts, and it saddens me that we are in an era when such experiences are harder to enjoy. Are there international Unitarian youth gatherings anywhere? And whatever happened to ministerial exchanges?

*

In more recent years I have enjoyed holidays in Berlin. The wall is now a tourist attraction and any boundary between east and west is barely discernible. We visited the renowned Checkpoint Charlie and bought a souvenir, what I hope is 'a piece of the true wall'. The Brandenburg Gate is a handsome, floodlit monument which visitors can stroll through, then pause near its corner to spend a moment in the Room of Silence. This gives you a break from the busy city and its dramatic history, perhaps to read the prayer of the United Nations:

> Oh Lord, our planet Earth is only a small star in space. It is our duty to transform it into a planet whose creatures are no longer tormented by war, hunger and fear, no longer senselessly divided by race, colour and ideology. Give us courage and strength to begin this task today so that our children and children's children shall one day carry the name of man with pride.

*

For this year's Remembrance Sunday, Cliff Reed, retired minster from Ipswich, composed a 'War Paternoster', which is half in German. My wife Celia tells of a conversation with a member of our Cross Street Chapel, Manchester, who had sold poppies outside an Aldi supermarket. A man came and put a coin in his box and said, "I, a German, buy a poppy from you, an Englishman, in England, outside a German supermarket!"

*

I'm grateful to Tony Rees for a copy of *Interchange*, an occasional journal of Edmund Kell Unitarian Church, Southampton. An article on South Africa by his wife Clare Rees tells this delightful story, "Doubtless apocryphal," she warns, "of a black driver being stopped by a man with a clipboard and being told that he is the 'winner' of a survey on seatbelt users. He is the first driver to have passed in an hour seen to be wearing a seat-belt, and consequently has been awarded a 500 Rand prize. The person from the Press in attendance then asks the driver how he plans to spend the prize money. "I think I'll probably buy a driving licence with it," he replies. The front seat passenger chips in saying, "Don't listen to him. He's drunk." Then the passenger in the back says, "I told you I didn't think you would get very far in a stolen car." Finally a voice from the boot asks, anxiously, "Are we over the border yet?" "Like most stories," Clare wisely concludes, "It says more than it tells."

November 2014

2015

Of dictionaries, nicknames and the kindertransport

2015

Of dictionaries, nicknames and the kindertransport

Of Unitarian trees, trains and crosswords

The love of crosswords is widespread, though many demur at cryptic puzzles, finding them too obscure to be coped with. In fact they are not nearly as difficult as many imagine, once the knack is understood. The meaning behind the meaning is an unfailing source of interest, as are the stories behind the stories.

A titbit of Unitarian-spotting, to get me through the festive season, popped up in the *Guardian* cryptic crossword on 12 December. 11 across: 'Narnia? Um, it is about Christian doctrine?'(11). Compiler John Tabraham, (pen-name *Qaos*) invites us here to make an anagram of 'Narnia it is um', with a question mark after 'Christian doctrine'. Does this mean he questions whether Unitarianism is Christian? His on-line biographical notes tell us he is a mathematician. No mention of his religious affiliation, though he also produces crosswords for the *Church Times*.

*

The recommended aid for *Guardian* crossword solvers is *Chambers English Dictionary*, so I was glad to be reminded by trustee Alan Ruston, who has been tidying the archives at Dr Williams's Library, that forty years ago a generous book grant enabled me to purchase a copy of *Chambers* for £3.50. He'll be pleased to learn that I still use it, at my bedside, in its dog-eared, battered condition. Among other virtues it is renowned for slipping in the odd bit of humour, defining an éclair as 'a cake, long in shape but short in duration'.

*

Bedside Chambers English Dictionary

Photo: John Midgley

Chambers also reminds me that 'reverend' is an adjective, not a noun. This means there is no such thing as 'a reverend', though it is frequently misused that way. There is nothing wrong with 'Rev. Mr' or 'Rev. Ms, Miss, Mrs, or Dr', as long as the adjective is linked to a noun. To be asked, 'Are you a reverend?' makes me wince. It's rather like asking a mayor, 'Are you a worshipful?' Most ministers these days are comfortable with first name terms, though it's perfectly polite to call a minister 'Mr' or one of the feminine equivalents. *Chambers* assures me that, 'Your

Reverence' is all right in Ireland, but 'playful' elsewhere, such as in *Dad's Army*. Alan Ruston calls me 'Reverend Sir,' but I'm sure he is just being playful.

*

The New Year task of disposing of the Christmas tree confronts us with the question as to whether to have a real tree or an artificial one. Too much artificiality demeans Christmas, while the thought of millions of living trees ravaged for a few days' pleasure sits very uncomfortably too. The delightful poem, *The Christmas Life*, by Wendy Cope was inspired by an 8-year old girl who said, "If you don't have a real tree you don't bring the Christmas life into the house." For the tree tradition in Britain we look to Prince Albert, Queen Victoria's consort, who brought the custom from Germany. A picture in the *Illustrated London News* of 1848 shows the royal family at Windsor Castle, gathered happily around a tree. This sparked the fashion. In the US, however, a different tradition prevails, crediting the introduction of Christmas trees there, not to a monarch, of course, but to a Unitarian minister, Rev. Charles Follen (1796-1840) and his wife, Eliza. His passions were religious freedom and the abolition of slavery, but he came to be known as 'the father of American Christmas trees.' A recently reproduced article from 2013, in the current issue of *UU World* tells us, 'The Follens' tree was nudged into history with the help of their friend and sister reformer, Harriet Martineau, who wrote about it in the popular magazine *Godey's Lady's Book*. Historians cite that tree, illuminated by Martineau's write-up, among the first Christmas trees in the United States.'

*

The autumn issue of the *Gaskell Society Newsletter* reports an event at Manchester Piccadilly station, the naming of a train as 'Elizabeth Gaskell'. A photo of society members, gathered on the platform for the occasion, includes some Unitarian faces, among them David and Helen Copley from Altrincham. Is this the only train to be named after a

Unitarian? Did Dickens ever get one? Some years ago, a previous columnist of the *Inquirer*, Alastair Ross, initiated a move to have one named after a former Principal of Manchester College Oxford, who was also a keen train-spotter. I don't think the move was successful, which is a pity. 'The Reverend Lancelot Garrard' would have looked wonderful on one of those magnificent, great, steam engines. Or how about 'Sir Tim Berners-Lee'?

*

January brings the annual Winter Walking Weekends at the Nightingale Centre, Great Hucklow. This year will be the twentieth year that the same David Copley has organised these popular weekends, though the tradition began some years earlier, led by David Dawson and family members. Winter attracts country walkers, and I wonder if any of them use natural navigation, a largely lost skill. Writer and broadcaster Tristan Gooley is leading its re-discovery, and has written extensively of signs and clues that enable him to make long treks across country without a compass or OS map. *The Natural Navigator* and *The Walker's Guide to Clues and Signs* (both pub. 2014) claim to teach how to find your way using not just the moon, sun and stars but spiders' webs, tennis courts and even puddles and ruts in the ground. Beginning with, "Now, which way am I facing? Ah, yes, there's a rainbow, so the sun *must* be behind me,' then, 'those trees are not symmetrical; they lean one way, so that must be south," you can conclude, "aha! now I know where I am," and enjoy your hikes much more. Do any Unitarians explore Derbyshire that way? The daily walks on these weekends end with jolly social activities in the evenings. I'd be glad to join in, if I can sit in the corner by a blazing fire, enjoying my crossword puzzle.

*

I can strongly recommend the film *The Imitation Game,* which tells of the brilliant life but tragic death of Alan Turing. A mathematician, like *Qaos,* he was the genius who led the team that cracked the *Enigma* code during WW2. He began his adventures in Bletchley Park through an enjoyment of crosswords. I'm neither mathematician nor code-breaker, but I enjoy crosswords, and I love éclairs.

January 2015

Worthy of a Pullet Surprise

More explorations into the meaning of words, both for fun and in more troubling situations. As minister poet the late Ric Masten put it, "When it comes to words, it's a miracle we communicate at all!"

The eternal endeavour to make sense of the English language led me, via a birthday book token, to *Spell It Out: The Singular Story of English Spelling* by David Crystal (2012). It helped me understand, for example, why the word ghost has an 'h' in it but goat doesn't. It's all to do with the history of English. There have always been waves of migration into the UK, bringing influences on the language, some of them seemingly welcomed, others not. Anglo-Saxon was one, and then came Latin, associated with Christian worship, giving it a sacred status and massive influence, which it still has. Then came French (1066). The 'ough' presence in words, variously pronounced (as in plough or cough) has always brought difficulties for learners, as does 'ight', as in bright light. Sprightly, however, originated from the French word *esperit*, and became sprite, but was considered somehow wrong for the adverb. The 'ight' was inserted to 'put it right' and give us sprightly. Awareness of this evolving history of our language and its spelling could influence our attitude towards immigration. Is there any resemblance between the impulse to fend off changes, in order to keep our language pure (as if it ever really was) and the desire to fend off immigration to keep Englishness and Britishness pure (as if they ever were)? And what about modern influences? Anybody for a balti, with naan and raita?

*

Do computer spell checkers help? They recognise words, but not meanings, as in this little poem:

I have a spelling checker,
It came with my PC.
It plane lee marks four my revue
Miss steaks aye can knot sea.

Eye ran this poem threw it,
Your sure reel glad two no.
Its vary polished in it's weigh.
My checker tolled me sew.   (Eckman and Zar)

A spell checker wouldn't spot anything wrong here, but people do get very anxious about it all. Employers will tell you that many a badly spelled job application has gone straight into the bin. Oh dear.

*

But there is fun in it too. A later chapter tells of sounds that we use that aren't words, as in this from Oscar Wilde:

CECILY: (taking dictation) Oh, don't cough Ernest. When one is dictating one should speak fluently and not cough. Besides, I don't know how to spell a cough (*The Importance of Being Earnest*, 1895, Act 2).

Crystal shows ways of spelling a cough, such as 'ahem' when one wishes to get attention. "Quite a few interjections are like this," he adds. "We make sounds at the back of our mouth to express various forms of disgust and these are only roughly indicated by spellings, such as *yuk*, *argh*, *ugh* and *blech*. We produce sounds using our lips, to express a range of emotions such as relief, astonishment and dismay, and write these down approximately as *phew, whew* and *pfff*. Think of *brrr* (I'm cold), *grrr* (I'm cross), *sh* (be quiet), or *pst* (I'm trying to get your attention surreptitiously). And new interjections have appeared, such as *mwah*, (for air kissing) and *phwoar...*"
Know what I mean? We'd better stop at this point. I wish I'd been taught some of this when I learned to write sermons.

*

I've often wished that the *Inquirer* had a professional cartoonist. The late Rod Dixon, a former minister, used the skill to great effect, and the appalling *Charlie Hebdo* incident in Paris has brought home the power that cartoons can have. Another book-token led me to *Swing under the Nazis: Jazz as a Metaphor for Freedom* by Mike Zwerin (1985). Hitler hated and banned jazz music, fearing its creativity and the freedom of expression it both needs and inspires. The book's cover has an appalling cartoon from a Nazi anti-jazz propaganda poster. It depicts a saxophonist, black with distinct monkey characteristics, wearing evening dress with bow tie and shiny silk top hat, plus a Star of David on his lapel. The propaganda is clear: Jazz is depraved music, arising from animal instincts and promoted by rich Jews. The book tells of the oppression of swing musicians in France during the WW2 occupation, and problems concerning collaboration arose:

> Collaboration - a dangerous word - suggesting that any contact between the two parties involved in occupation represents a sort of treason on the part of the occupied. Was a taxi driver a collaborator when he drove a German? Was a waiter when he served one? A musician when he played for one? When music made Gestapo officers in the audience feel pleasure, did this perhaps make them more reluctant to inflict pain? Is this collaboration or resistance?

*

A gem from a second-hand bookshop gave me the autobiographical *Chasing Shadows* by Hugo Gryn (1930–1996), Auschwitz-Birkenau concentration camp survivor, Reform rabbi and popular broadcaster. I recall hearing him in a confrontation with a member of an ultra-right, holocaust denying group. "*Look* at me!" said Hugo. "Look me in the face and say it didn't happen! I was there. Look at me now and say it didn't happen!"

*

A story from his book leapt out. During his boyhood in Carpathia in Eastern Europe, Hugo's family employed a German housemaid who also taught him German, until she announced she was leaving. She had espoused Nazi ideology and could no longer work for Jews or live with them. Hugo felt rejected and hurt. A few weeks later they learned that 'the Fraulein' was ill, lonely and in hospital. Hugo was astonished and angry to see his mother pack a basket of cakes and fruit and the young woman's favourite recipes to take to her. "She's a sick woman, and perhaps dying," said my mother, "and for a long time she was good to you."

The Yiddish word for her attitude is *'R'akm'án's'*. I hope I've spelt it correctly. It means compassion.

January 2015

What's in a nickname? More than you think

The question of our denominational name, and the names of other organisations as well as people and their titles, raises ponderings about instinctive associations, some of which can be deeply troubling. Yet for us there is a reluctance to change names, though others are prepared to do it.

Congratulations to the Right Rev. Libby Lane on her February appointment as the first woman bishop in the Church of England. More precisely, she is a suffragan bishop, a strange term that has a whiff of ecclesiastical obscurity about it. It means that she is a subsidiary bishop, able to function in a smaller diocese. There seems to be no complaint that it is a secondary role; one assumes she will make it to full status bishop in due course. Nor does anyone seem to mind that she is known by a childhood nickname instead of Elizabeth. I wonder about nicknames. They usually indicate affection for the person concerned, but in the case of someone in a significant leadership position, doesn't a nickname risk a loss of gravitas? And has anyone else, besides me, found themselves, at the sound of her name, bursting into the chorus of one of the Beatles' jollier songs? Did her congregants 'There beneath the blue suburban skies' of Hale, in Cheshire, react in the same way?

*

The use of a helpful or unhelpful name prompts me again to ponder the mystery of our Unitarian name. There are plenty who are convinced we should change it, to make it easier for newcomers to understand who we are. I'm not so sure, and the other denominations don't seem too troubled by their names either. To the complete outsider, what does Anglicanism or even the Church of England actually mean? Or Methodist, Congregationalist or Baptist? Imagine someone writing a book, 'Methodist? What's that?' Quakers seem content to stick with what was originally a derisory jibe, perhaps because their formal name, Religious Society of Friends sounds like a friendly society, which is not quite the same thing. Someone once commented that United Reformed sounds like a football team that has been taken over by a press magnate. A local evangelical Christian church, formerly Carmel Pentecostal Church and latterly Skipton Christian Fellowship, has just changed its name to The Champions Church. Champions at what, one wonders? Changing their name?

*

This prompts me to look at football clubs in a similar way. Soccer is sometimes described as a religion, but that's an idea that shouldn't be pressed too far. Some soccer clubs have very strange names. The ones labelled for their city or town are obvious enough, until one discovers that many of the players and even managers do not come from that place, or even this country and several of the famous ones are owned by millionaires from overseas. And Arsenal could be anywhere. Titles like Rovers or Rangers are barely comprehensible, after which things start to become very obscure. Albion? Hotspur? Wednesday? Academicals? And how did Argyle manage to slip down from Scotland to the south coast of England? I don't ever remember a football club changing its name in an effort to attract more fans or to gain more points to get a higher position in the league; or should that be 'The con- ference'? Why 'conference'? There are probably historical reasons for all of these nomenclatures, and stories to tell as to how they came about. Just like the denominations. Football club devotees seem loyal enough despite these obscure names, and I can imagine howls of protest at any suggestion of a change.

*

The names of places sometimes attract unfortunate associations, hard to shake off. My wife Celia tells me that in her childhood, the neighbouring town of Bacup was frequently described as the place 'where they look with their fingers'. More seriously, it is still difficult to mention the delightful Scottish town of Lockerbie without thinking of the terrible air disaster of 1988. In fact, the unforgettable way that Lockerbie townsfolk responded to that tragedy, giving help and hospitality to visiting relatives of victims, ought to attract nothing but praise. A recently released film that has attracted high commendation from the critics has a place name for its title. For those with strong memories of the civil rights movement in the US, the name Selma resonates loudly enough to know instantly what the movie is all about. The story has a particular resonance for Unitarians, it being the occasion of the murder of a Unitarian Universalist minister. In the film there is a fleeting appearance of a thin, bespectacled man wearing a bow tie. That is James Reeb, a modern martyr. Unitarian Universalist Viola Luizzo is also seen, and she too was murdered by racists in Alabama.

*

Would I ever want to visit a place with a name resonant with bigotry and cruelty? I have taken a summer holiday in Poland which included a visit to Auschwitz, this year being the 70th anniversary of its liberation. Now there's a name with strong associations. Given the opportunity, I hope I would visit Selma too, as I'm sure there are plenty of kind and decent people there. There doesn't seem to be a Unitarian Universalist congregation, but there is one in Birmingham, not too far away. That is a name that resonates with me, as Birmingham England is the place of my birth.

Back in my boyhood there were countless immigrants in that mighty, industrial city, from commonwealth countries as well as Ireland. Many of them gave a much needed boost to the staffing of public services. I have no recollection of serious race riots in the streets where I lived, though troubles around a notorious election campaign in nearby Smethwick were appalling. Often we tried to deal with issues of community relations and integration by telling jokes, some of which now make me squirm a little.

"How can you recognise a true Brummie these days?" we asked. "By the spray of shamrock in his turban." One that feels a little less uncomfortable asked the question, "Why did job-seeking immigrants want to go to live in Birmingham England rather than Birmingham Alabama? In Birmingham Alabama they had to sit at the back of the bus. In Birmingham England they got to drive one!"

March 2015

The only thing missing was the Doctor

Choosing a suitable venue for our denomination's annual meetings is no easy task. Once there, however we enjoy re-connecting with co-religionists from far and near, celebrating their joys and anniversaries and even indulging in some gentle teasing.

Again the GA chose a luxurious venue for its Annual Meetings. What our austere puritan forbears would make of this is hard to imagine. Stepping inside the Birmingham Hilton Metropole Hotel, close by the NEC and Birmingham International airport, it took me a moment to get my bearings. So big! Large rooms, long corridors in all directions. It reminded me of somewhere…

…I know, the TARDIS! I wandered around, taking it all in, and then, aha, what's that aroma? Ah, yes, a swimming pool. And here are some folk in towelling bathrobes. I expect some of our livelier delegates will enjoy early morning dips. And here come some healthy keep-fit types on their way towards the Ocean Rooms Spa, wearing very few clothes, though the less they wear, the more fashion conscious they seem to be. The spa promises "to rejuvenate your body and mind with a range of treatments for your wellbeing." And does that notice really say, "Beauty is available at the LivingWell Health Centre"? I must remember to call in and get some, though it's rather expensive, like the drinks in the bar. As for my well-being, I decided to put my trust in the various worship services during the meetings, and was not disappointed.

*

What else to discover? The hotel is a venue for office events, reunions and family parties. I met entertainers dressed as characters from *The Wizard of Oz*, though there was no yellow brick road. And what's this? A Dalek! Standing in the corner, large as life and so big! So I really am in the TARDIS! Should I be scared and hide behind the sofa like my children did when they were small? Is Dr Who here? I thought this place was supposed to relax my well-being. It was time to move on and settle down to business.

*

We love marking anniversaries. Our keynote speaker was Rev. Jill McAllister from the US, with a ministry in Oregon combined with work as senior programme consultant for the International Council of Unitarians and Universalists. This year is the 20th anniversary of its founding, a UK initiative. Jill enthralled us with ideas and exercises to test our prejudices, or at least our inclinations to stereotype people without realising we are doing it. "Someone pointed out to me a guy who worked as a forester, you know, a woodsman, a lumberjack. Then they told me that he is Jewish. 'What?' I said. 'Jewish? How can he be Jewish?' But then, why not? Why shouldn't he be Jewish? So, why did this shock me?"

It all comes down to understanding our preconceptions, and how they get in the way of dealing with our differences. She was a stimulating and refreshing presence at our meetings, and gladly received our congratulations on ICUU's twenty years of growth, particularly in Africa. Can we imagine French speaking African Unitarians? We shall have to get used to it, and find out where Burundi is.

*

A linked anniversary is 100 years of the incorporation of the British and Foreign Unitarian Association (B&FUA) a forerunner of the GA. It still exists and manages lots of valuable trusts. Strange to think that back in the last century, British Unitarians were wealthy enough to send funds to foreign and commonwealth countries to promote the cause. A longstanding worker for the B&FUA is Alan Ruston, who was honoured at the meetings by the Unitarian Historical Society, also one hundred years old. Their latest issue of *Transactions* is a festschrift to Alan, that's a special collection of historical essays to honour him for all his work.

*

At that same meeting the Yorkshire Unitarian Union slipped in a plug for its 200th anniversary publication, *Roots and Wings*, which includes a brief history of the YUU and some contemporary worship materials. Included is mention of a now closed congregation which thrived for some years in the Yorkshire town of Idle. This is the place that is renowned for the Idle Workingmen's Club and the Idle Women's Institute, whose worldwide aficionados delight in showing off their membership cards. It always saddens me when congregations close, but the loss of this one touches me especially. I would love to have been able to tell the world I was the Idle Unitarian minister.

*

The business meetings were led by our President, Marion Baker, who also had an anniversary. On the last day of her Presidential year, she and husband Ernest celebrated their 48th wedding anniversary. Yes, it was April 1st which lent itself to appropriate remarks, most of them mercifully unspoken. The daily paper of these meetings, the *GAZette*, published, on that same day, appropriately, results of "an undercover investigation" into proposed changes in our denominational structure. We are to have an archbishop and a network of bishops and deans. Our archbishop designate, Rev. Dr Ann Peart, was pictured in her new regalia, crook and all. I felt sorry that this was an April fool spoof. She looked rather good in it.

*

After a few days here, engrossed in the series of meetings and worship, it all ended in good spirits, though a number of delegates reported that they felt cut off from the real world. We could have been anywhere in time and space. This sensation, and the hotel's carefully sterilised air-conditioned atmosphere began to get to me too. I'd rather go to our Nightingale Centre, which, we learned in their annual report, now proudly boasts a Visit England 4star rating, plus bicycle shed.
  Better than a TARDIS, any time.

April 2015

To Hull, Hell and Halifax (and Brum)

Paying visits to one or two of our congregations from time to time tells me a little about how they fare in their particular context. Some of these visits take me down Memory Lane, others reveal changes and events going on around them into which they can make their contributions. Some additional reflections say something about old movies and revised dictionaries.

I really had thought that the old saying, 'From Hull, Hell and Halifax, Good Lord deliver us!' was now largely forgotten. On a recent visit, however, both the ticket clerk at the train station and a chatty fellow passenger gave a wry smile and comment suggesting that Hull is not exactly a desirable place for a weekend. The jibe is of uncertain origin, but Hull once had a notoriously severe prison and Halifax a reputation for public executions. But today, Hull is gearing itself up to become City of Culture for 2017. A photograph exhibition in its central library promoted its friendly, multicultural community. A recent addition to the city is the Unitarian church's lay pastor Ralph Catts, a proud and energetic Australian. Finding that there were no local plans to celebrate Anzac Day, and knowing that this was the centenary of that disastrous

Gallipoli landing that the day marks, Ralph laid on a memorial service. It attracted a full congregation including representatives of the city, the Australian High Commission in London and a local veterans' support centre. Wreaths were laid, in the church and at the nearby cenotaph. ITV news reported the event with scenes of the service and an interview with Ralph. No mention of the word Unitarian, but as someone commented, "No-one would mistake that for a parish church!"

*

A visit to Birmingham, for the Induction service of Rev. Winnie Gordon, gave a similar experience of multi-cultural activity. Driving past my former Unitarian Church, now a Sikh Gurdwara, I witnessed a crowd gathered around their bright orange flagpole in preparation for its ceremonial raising. This was to mark Vaisakhi, the anniversary of the birth of Sikhism as a collective faith, in 1699. In the city centre a major Sikh publicity activity provided literature and a friendly young Sikh woman to answer questions. She told me, "Yes, we have had equality for women, including women priests, for a long time." Inevitably there was food available. Sikhs love to feed people, and spoke of a food pantry and hot food kitchen they hold there, offering help to up to a 150 hungry and homeless, every night. What would the city do without them, one wonders.

*

A *Guardian* piece in February leapt out at me. It mentioned two of my pre-occupations, nature and words. Travel writer and naturalist Robert McFarlane reported that a few years ago, a new edition of the *Oxford Junior Dictionary* was published. "A sharp-eyed reader noticed that there had been a culling of words concerning nature." These were words that the publishers "no longer felt to be relevant to modern-day childhood. The deletions included *acorn, adder, ash, beech, bluebell, buttercup, catkin, conker, cowslip, cygnet, dandelion, fern, hazel, heather … mistletoe… otter…willow.* The words taking their place in the new edition included *attachment, blog, broadband, celebrity, chatroom, cut-and-paste, MP3player* and *voicemail…* I was dismayed. For blackberry, read Blackberry."

One wonders what religious terms were included or excluded for the benefit of junior readers. Has *spirituality* replaced *religion?* Is *Unitarian* there? What about *multi-faith* or *multicultural?*

*

Anniversary corner. Cinema giant Orson Welles was born just 100 years ago. Two of his films stand out, one containing a challenge to liberally minded peace lovers. As Harry Lime, in *The Third Man*, he tosses out what is surely a classic piece of cynicism: "You know what the fellow said – in Italy, for thirty years under the Borgias, they had warfare, terror, murder and bloodshed, but they produced Michelangelo, Leonardo da Vinci and the Renaissance. In Switzerland, they had brotherly love, they had five hundred years of democracy and peace – and what did that produce? The cuckoo clock."

Oh, dear. Would that make a good topic for a discussion group on spirituality and peace?

Then there was *Citizen Kane,* in which Welles played a press magnate, loosely based on Randolph Hearst. There is a strong psychoanalytic undercurrent to this film. Viewers are invited to ponder the influence of traumatic childhood experiences, and discern the meaning of Kane's deathbed utterance, "Rosebud!" Any Unitarian connection? Only that the newspaper that this media giant owned was called *The Inquirer.* A mere coincidence, or did the film-makers scout around for a good name, find us and help themselves?

*

Meanwhile, back in Hull Central Library the Books for Sale section proved tempting. I felt troubled by the thought that a library was flogging off its stock, wondering if it was a victim of public spending cuts. *A Poet in the Family* by Danny Abse (1923-2014) proved irresistible to this lover of autobiographies. Abse's career was in medicine as a chest clinic specialist, but his vocation was poetry. He himself made that interesting distinction. Career or vocation? How do Unitarian ministers describe their work? He was certainly familiar with at least one, as he was often to be seen at Golders Green Unitarians for poetry evenings during the late Keith Gilley's days there. Born in Wales to a Jewish family, he had an older brother Leo, a politician and another brother Walter, an eminent psychoanalyst. He writes affectionately of his childhood in Swansea, which brought its own multi-cultural difficulties for a Jewish child who somehow ended up being sent to a Roman Catholic school. He was excused religious education classes and morning assembly, but his puzzlement remained. One day he went home and asked, "Mum, who is this Jesus Price?"

*

All of which prompts me to think that there has been some progress in community relations over the years. The preparatory publicity for the City of Culture 2017 states: "Unique, quirky and eccentric, Hull is a warm, inventive and colourful place that has a remarkable story to tell and a people that are happy to share it." Philip Larkin's statue, striding across the station concourse, will attract attention. The strapline given to the Library's photo exhibition reads Honour Diversity, Promote Community, Love Humanity. Hull Unitarians will surely feel comfortable enough, joining in with that in 2017.

May 2015

Of blackberries, Magna Carta and Puritans

Anything to do with freedom, justice and democracy is bound to attract attention, so the anniversary of Magna Carta certainly merited a visit. Also, it is good and flattering to receive responses to topics previously mentioned.

I was glad of a springtime holiday break which included a stroll in what is sometimes described as the most famous meadow in the world. Runnymede meadow, alongside the Thames, is where Magna Carta was signed just 800 years ago. A distant Unitarian connection here. The meadow was rescued and gifted to the National Trust in 1931 by Cara, the first Lady Fairhaven. Who's she? The daughter of self-made millionaire industrialist Henry Huttleston Rogers, described as a principal in the Esso Empire. Among numerous benefactions, he funded the fabulous, cathedral-like Fairhaven Unitarian Universalist church in Massachusetts, where I had the delight of a ministerial exchange in 1987. The Magna Carta Memorial in Runnymede resembles a small classical Greek temple. Alas, it was covered with scaffolding, undergoing cleaning ready for the great anniversary day in June, but the inscription was clear: Symbol of Freedom Under Law.

*

I chatted with a couple of folk on a nearby bench. The man told me that when he was a boy, all of this area was overgrown with brambles. He and his pals used to come blackberrying.

"All pretty wild, then?" I asked.

"Yes," he replied, "though there was always a Warden on duty."

"To chase you away from the blackberries?"

He smiled and said, "One time, we came and put a little tent up here, and the Warden came along and said, 'You can take that down!'"

"Spoilsport!" I said.

"Well," he grinned. "We just waited until he'd gone away and then we put it back up again!"

Exercising their freedom under law, perhaps. Cheered me up, no end.

*

The American presence at Runnymede is strong. The American Bar Association funded the Memorial, and close by stands an oak tree planted by the Queen in soil from Jamestown Virginia, the first permanent English settlement in the New World. It commemorates the bicentenary of the Constitution of the US, as historians are sure that the freedoms proclaimed in Magna Carta resonate through to that founding US document. Higher up a nearby hill stands a memorial to John F Kennedy, on a plot of land actually given to the USA, and is therefore officially American soil. It has some words from JFK's inaugural address: "Let every nation know... that we shall pay any price, bear any burden, meet any hardship, support any friend, oppose any foe, in order to assure the survival and success of liberty." Stirring words, though on reflection perhaps raising a slightly niggling question: *Any* price? Really?

*

Good to spot a news item with another American connection, and a sort of Unitarian first. British born Sir Tim Berners-Lee, creator of the World Wide Web, lives in the US, but his fame has now been recognised by the National Portrait Gallery, London, in the form of a bronze statue. Apart from photographs, it is the first commissioned portrait, and depicts him striding purposefully forward, with his leather rucksack in which he carries his laptop. He won't be alone. The Gallery is always worth a visit and has plenty of other Unitarians, though not all on display. I have seen James Martineau and Charles Dickens there, and their website catalogue mentions Florence Nightingale, Joseph Priestley, Adrian Boult and many more.

*

I'm grateful for feedback. Annette Percy writes: "Your item about the new edition of the *Oxford Junior Dictionary* and the things that had been deleted worries me. I was recently standing at the bus stop outside a wild bit of Clissold Park when a child said to her mother, 'Look at the flowers!' Her Mum said disparagingly, 'They're only dandelions.' It always pleases me to remember that Primary school children in the Czech Republic spend a week each year with their class at 'a School in Nature'. Those youngsters would be able to identify masses of trees and their fruits and lots of wild flowers as well as numerous birds."

*

Two responses to the saying or refrain, 'From Hell, Hull and Halifax, good Lord deliver us!' quoted last month. Rev. Phillip Hewett writes from Canada: "I was always under the impression that what you quoted was an old seamen's saying, reflecting the view that going to port in Hull or Halifax, Nova Scotia, was tantamount to going to hell!" Michael Tracey from Hull UK writes that historically there may well be a sort of Unitarian link. "Apparently the refrain refers to the severe measures adopted by the leading citizens in the treatment of beggars and vagrants and the control of vice. Vice in this context meant anything to which the Puritans objected. The majority of the leading citizens were Puritans, Leonard Chamberlain was one of them. In the latter years of the 17th century he, along with the other members of the Bowl Alley Lane Chapel and other leading citizens of the town founded the Society for the Reformation of Manners because of: 'The abounding Sin and Wickedness of the present Age and Place in which we live'. The minute book still survives today. It records a long list of prosecutions, the majority relatively trivial such as drinking at unreasonable hours, swearing an oath, travelling on the Lord's Day with fish. Swearing was the most common offence for which one could be fined one shilling. Puritans not only felt the responsibility for keeping themselves unstained from the world but also for controlling moral behaviour in society at large."

Michael chairs the Leonard Chamberlain Trust, which funds the Unitarian congregation and other worthy causes. I have no thoughts of becoming a seaman but wouldn't mind a visit Nova Scotia. And on future visits to Hull I must remember not to carry fish on a Sunday, and always keep a few shillings handy to pay any fines.

June 2015

'Money - that's ethics; sex - that's morals'

Matters of life and death are always worth exploring, but one is a little reluctant to do so when they include questions concerning evil and dead bodies. The mood can always be lifted, however, by some thoughts about words and language.

News of the death of horror film actor Christopher Lee prompts me to consider, again, the mystery of evil, something Unitarians do not dwell on very much. Indeed, you may have already stopped reading. I know of no Unitarian literature that explores this subject, and when it is called 'sin' we usually turn over the page, preferring to affirm the goodness in people.

I've tried to understand evil, not by watching supposedly entertaining supernatural horror films, but by focusing on the real thing. What is evil? A real, spiritual force in the world, in which case where does it come from? Or is it simply the absence of good? Or are there always psychological explanations for evil behaviour? Are evil people mad? For movies about real life evil, as against the Hammer horror supernatural, I watch depictions of the mafia, such as *Goodfellas* or the *Godfather* trilogy. These last star my favourite actor Al Pacino, whose evil characters simmer with dark forebodings, until real human rage bursts out. Nobody 'does' anger like Al Pacino. I am impressed by his performances, but not much wiser as to the nature of evil.

*

I recall hearing of a television interview with a so-called mafia boss. The words 'ethical' and 'moral' frequently cropped up, until the interviewer asked, "Do you know the difference between ethics and morals?"

"Oh, sure," the mafioso replied. "If it's to do with money, that's ethics. If it's to do with sex, that's morals." Wrong, but amusing and interesting.

I recently came across a quotation from the late Kurt Vonnegut (1922–2007), writer and novelist whom we like to claim as a Unitarian Universalist. "There is no reason good can't triumph over evil, if only angels will get organised along the lines of the mafia." An intriguing thought, but he surely recognised the internal contradiction. Mafia organisations are characterised by lies and concealment. Angels operating that way would be overcome by evil, not overcome it.

*

Horror movies often include gory depictions of corpses and skeletons. Are Unitarians interested in such things? Sensitive readers need not fear to read on. Some intriguing correspondence in the *Guardian* in June raised the question as to what happened to the remains of Thomas Paine (1737-1809) the great civil libertarian, political activist and revolutionary. There is no official burial place for him, and writer Gavin Jacobson recently repeated the widely held view that "William Cobbett (1763-1835) critic-turned-disciple of Paine's, exhumed the body and took it with him to England, where he hoped to honour the patriot with a superior memorial. But when Cobbett died in 1835, the remains were still among his possessions, unburied; what happened to them next is unknown."

We can't claim Tom Paine as a Unitarian but there were connections. One correspondent (Michael Bush, *London*) replied:

> Gavin Jacobson says nothing is known of Thomas Paine's remains following William Cobbett's death in 1835. In fact, the remains passed immediately to Cobbett's neighbour George West and then to Cobbett's old friend Benjamin Tilly, who acted as their guardian from 1844 until his own death in 1869. It is also known that eventually the remains became dispersed, with the skull acquired by the Rev. Robert Ainslie in the 1850s and finding its way to Australia in the 1890s; the brain returned to Paine's original burial place in New Rochelle, New York state, around 1900; and most of the skeleton acquired by Alexander Gordon following Tilly's death, and given a secret burial in the mid-1870s, probably in the Manchester area where Gordon worked as a Unitarian minister.

*

Did Rev. Alexander Gordon, the great scholar-principal at Unitarian College, collect relics? What did he do with Tom Paine's skeleton? Speculation has been rife. There is even a folk song, *Tom Paine's Bones*. It is possible that they are among those that have lain for years alongside Cross Street Unitarian Chapel in Manchester, though that's speculation on my part. The former burial ground there has been recently disturbed by the laying of tracks for Manchester's *Metrolink* tram system. Removing and re-interring the bodies is taking a frustratingly long time, causing serious disruption to the life of the city centre generally and our congregation in particular.

*

Cross Street Chapel's graves have been disturbed before, for the rebuilding of the Chapel in the 1990s. A large number of bodies were removed and re-interred, including that of the founder-minister Rev. Henry Newcome (1627-1695). Some of the graves were below the building, where the underground car park is now to be found. During my ministry there, as the rebuilding of the chapel was being completed, the clerk of works for the project, a seemingly down-to-earth rational Mancunian, shared his troubled thoughts about disturbing the dead. "Several of my workmen have suffered some mysterious illnesses while working on this job," he told me. "I can't help thinking we're doing the wrong thing." I smiled, and tried to reassure him, saying that I had encountered several ghosts down there. "But they were all friendly, they were Unitarians." I said.

It didn't seem to work.

*

Away from such talk for a holiday in the beautiful but sweltering Mosel Valley. I'm not good at learning enough of a foreign language to be useful, so draw comfort from Mark Twain. In *The Awful German Language* (1880) he admits that learning it tormented him, especially declensions. "I heard a Californian student in Heidelberg say, in one of his calmer moods, that he would rather decline two drinks than one German adjective." As for nouns, "In German it is true that by some oversight of the inventor of the language, a woman is female but a wife (*weib*) is not – which is unfortunate. A wife, here, has no sex; she is neuter; so, according to the grammar, a fish is *he*, his scales are *she* but a fishwife is neither."

I wonder, would this help, or add confusion, in the formulation of same-sex wedding ceremonies?

July 2015

Modest heroes are unsullied by ego

The plight of migrants, desperate people making their way across Europe to escape war-torn homelands, resonated clearly with memories of the man credited with enabling the rescue of children during WW2. The need for inspiring and uplifting songs and hymns, to motivate the impulses to help, seems worthy of a mention.

I love stories about modest heroes, who discreetly get on with some tremendous endeavour, then quietly walk away. Such a one was Sir Nicholas Winton, for whom obituaries appeared in July. He organized the rescue of trainloads of children from Czechoslovakia on the eve of WW2, in an operation later known as the Czech kindertransport ('children transportation'). Winton found homes in the UK for them and arranged their safe passage. As part of the process, the UK government demanded a £50 warranty for each child. The *Guardian* obituary includes the following astonishing paragraph:

> Frustrated by the slowness of the British authorities, Winton made newspaper appeals and personally organised the children's placements, with no time for checking suitability or haggling over who should go where. As the situation in Czechoslovakia grew more desperate following the German occupation of the entire country in March 1939, he took to forging the Home Office entry permits. That summer eight rail transports were conducted. A ninth Kindertransport, which was due to leave on 1 September 1939 with 250 more children, was cancelled by the Germans, and most of those who would have been on board were subsequently transported to concentration camps. Nevertheless, Winton and his colleagues had saved at least 664 children: 561 of them Jewish, 52 Unitarians, 34 Catholics and 17 others.

Winton was no publicity-seeker and was only recognized with a knighthood decades later. I am grateful to Roger Crosskey of Bessels Green for spotting what may be a forgotten bit of Unitarian history hidden in this story. Does anyone know what happened to those

Unitarian children? Presumably they were from our congregation in Prague (where there was a large Sunday school). Were they placed with UK Unitarians? Or were they perhaps Jews in disguise, as it is known that Rev. Dr Norbert Capek accepted Jews into his congregation, to give them cover and time to plan their escape.

*

Some small clues have come from a recent visit to the lovely Old Meeting House, Tenterden in Kent. Retired minister David Skelton drew my attention to a memorial plaque there to former minister Rev. Walter Walsh and his wife. They are believed to have helped people from war-torn Czechoslovakia, though the details are not known. Also, a snippet from the Association of Jewish Refugees' *Journal* of April 2009 quotes Sir Nicholas: "I went out round the camps with Eleanor Rathbone at the time, and the Reverend Rosalind Lee, who was the head of the Unitarian Church and the people in the camps were those people who'd fled from Sudetenland and hadn't got either friends or relatives to stay with and they were just put into camps." In *The Wine of Life* (1991) Rev. John McLachlan told of two months he spent in 1938, helping Rosalind Lee in Prague.

*

There is a Jewish blessing, usually given to a bereaved person: 'I wish you a long life.' Though a non-practising son of Jewish parents, Sir Nicholas must have heard that blessing offered many times. For him it came true. He died peacefully aged 106 years.

*

Exploring the good long life of former *Inquirer* company secretary, the late Kate Taylor, I enjoyed her eyebrow-raising autobiography, *Not So Merry Wakefield* (2005). The somewhat misleading title alludes to the frequent appellation 'merry' to her home city. Her personal history was a mix of struggle and substantial achievements. She won numerous school prizes, usually National Savings Stamps, presented on speech days, when they sang the school song:

Hear the ancient watchword ringing,
Each for all and all for God.

Perhaps this inspired her through many tough years, though ironically, she made no bones about calling herself an atheist.

*

Many readers could, I expect, stand and sing their school song, word perfect. Belonging to a past era, these earnest anthems tend to raise smiles, even derisory grins. One wonders about their influence. They were meant to be uplifting, even visionary. My wife Celia well remembers Todmorden Grammar School song, and half-laughs as she holds up her head and sings the opening lines:

Clean are the hands if the heart be unsullied,
Strong are the arms if the courage be high.

"I love that word, 'unsullied'", I tell her. I cannot think where else but in a school song it might be used. Perhaps I'm envious. My school (now long closed) didn't have a song. There are many such anthems, the most famous being *Gaudeamus Igitur*, also *Forty Years On* from Harrow school. It gave a title to the Alan Bennett play about a public school, described by critics as "nostalgic and astringent, elegiac and unsettling".

*

The nearest I ever got to such corporate uplift was when, on the last day of term before the summer holidays, we sang, with almost raucous joy, 'Lord, dismiss us with thy blessing'. Then, on the first day of a new term, with scarcely disguised gloom, 'Lord, behold us with thy blessing, Once again assembled here'.

Better still, for me, was the hymn written for the Unitarian Young

People's League, sung for many years at annual meetings and rallies. Rev. Arthur Vallance, a Sedbergh School pupil, understood the uplifting power of a good tune, chose *Little Cornard* then composed 'Lord of the Wondrous Earth' (*Hymns for Living* 1). It had the desired effect on me as a teenager, in the Old Chapel, Great Hucklow:

> Creator Spirit touch with power
> Our youthful wills this worship hour.

Somewhat dated, it nonetheless holds up well, calling for courage and willingness to serve:

> Daring the truth to speak,
> E'en to the worldly-wise,
> Swift to defend the weak,
> Eager for enterprise.

*

I wonder if the Kindertransport children had songs to keep their spirits up. He won't have known the UYPL hymn, but did Nicholas Winton have such sentiments in mind when, 'swift to defend the weak' he organized those train journeys and, 'eager for enterprise', forged entry permits to ensure the children's safety?

August 2015

Old school ties and church ties

Again it felt flattering to receive further observations from readers about a topic raised previously. The implied questions are about what inspired young people towards creative and even heroic activities in their lives. Matters of dress code and appearance always raise smiles and eyebrows.

It has been a delight to learn from colleagues and friends that the school they attended had a school song, sometimes specially composed, sung on speech days and prize-giving, and fondly remembered. I mentioned this in a previous issue, noting particularly the use in one instance of the word 'unsullied'. It suggests the school's sometimes forlorn endeavour to promote purity of heart in its pupils. Sure enough, retired minister Penny Johnson responded with news that her school song contained that very word. Others mention a song that attempted to inspire loyalty, as in Elizabeth Birtles's memory of singing, from a Unitarian-Quaker foundation school:

> School that we love, we pledge to thee,
> And in our hearts enshrine-ed be,
> To hand on to posterity
> *Fideliter, Fortiter, Feliciter.*

She grinned as she told me this, as did Cliff Reed, when he pomped up his voice and sang,

> Strive for the highest, friend with friend,
> Strive for the highest, on to the end!

Another friend mentioned *I vow to thee my country*, seen as the epitome of patriotism, always a debateable virtue. Another mentioned *These things shall be, a loftier race than e'er the world hath known shall rise*, which has appeared in Unitarian hymnals in the past, though with one verse deleted that I can remember singing at my school:

> Woman shall be man's mate and peer,
> In all things wise and fair and good,
> Still wearing on her brow the crown
> Of sinless, sacred motherhood.

Nicky Jenkins (minister of our church in Chorlton) remembers that at her school they always sang *Non nobis domine*. This has a complex and interesting history. Based on a psalm, it was allegedly the anthem of the Knights Templar, and, again allegedly after the victory at Agincourt, the 600th anniversary of which is being celebrated this year, it was sung by King Henry V and his soldiers. It features in the film version of

Shakespeare's play of that name. Tradition has it that it should be sung while on one's knees, as the virtue it extols is self-abasement. No wonder Nicky looked uncomfortable when she told me about it.

*

One wonders what exactly these songs were intended to do. Much of their power is their tunes, which appeal to the emotions, at least as much as do the words. So I was surprised to read in *Classic Ephemera, a Musical Miscellany* (2009) the origin of the oft-quoted question, 'Why should the devil have all the good tunes?' It is usually attributed to Martin Luther, sometimes to General Booth of the Salvation Army. This book claims it originated with Roland Hill (1795–1879) the man credited with originating the basic concepts of the modern postal service, beginning with the invention of the penny black postage stamp. He was a Unitarian and his family were friendly with Joseph Priestley. Born in Kidderminster, he moved into Birmingham and founded a school. I wonder if it had a school song with a devilishly good tune?

*

I had thought that the phenomenon of the salon, a gathering of men and women to discuss and debate social and political issues of the day, was a thing of the past. Not so. I learn from Rev. Phil Waldron that at least one such salon exists, and has recently met at our Ullet Road Church, Liverpool. He found the debate thoroughly enjoyable and stimulating. "I left feeling that my I.Q. was now about ten points higher!" he said. The topic discussed was a book by Sunderland University lecturer, Dr Kevin Yuill: *Assisted Suicide: The Liberal, Humanist Case Against Legalization* (2013). Now that the move to change the legislation on assisted suicide has failed in the House of Commons, I mention this only to remind readers that it is easy to categorise people mistakenly. Any notion that religious conservative types are against the change, and liberal humanist types are for it, is challenged in this book's very title.

*

Among the many miles of newsprint on the Labour Party's new leader there is much about his casual appearance. He is not alone among politicians that are rarely to be seen wearing a necktie these days. Matters of fashion are something of a mystery to me. I frequently wear a necktie, as much for warmth and convenience as anything else. I have even been seen wearing one whilst doing the gardening, having popped out for an hour or so to mow the lawn, without taking the trouble to change into overalls.

It would be a pity if neckties vanish altogether, as they have served Unitarians well, displaying our flaming chalice symbol. I have a number of them in various colours, acquired over the years, dating from the earliest, 1960s version. This, alas, caused some confusion as it had many small chalices on, which looked like tiny aeroplanes and prompted questions as to which branch of the RAF the wearer belonged. Currently, our GA Visibility Strategy Group no longer produces such things, but an enterprising Martin Fieldhouse has taken up the challenge and produced a supply, bearing a single, modern version of the flaming chalice.

*

I am among a number of ministers who long ago replaced the clerical collar with a plain white necktie, worn against a white shirt. This has aroused some comment, as dress code matters for ministers always do, with special problems for women ministers. The white colour of my tie is something of a nod towards the clerical collar, while avoiding any priestly connotations. However, I always take it off immediately after conducting a service, to avoid spilling anything on it during coffee hour. I can't vouch for the state of my heart, but I want my tie to remain unsullied.

September 2015

Cemetery friends and women ministers

The theme of women in the ministry emerges, this time to indicate progress. Other excursions back in time suggest that Unitarian sympathies do not change so very much, or at least show signs of being repeated.

Travelling to our Nightingale Centre at Great Hucklow always lifts my spirits. I once heard a colleague describe the sensation. As his journey there took him into the Derbyshire hills he always found himself hum--ing the opening section of Beethoven's *Pastoral* symphony. "Good heavens!" I said, "I thought it was just *me* that did that." Beethoven tells us that the piece depicts the awakening of happy feelings when arriving in the countryside. The continuing improvements in the centre's amenities aroused happiness in me too. So too did the sight of ministerial colleagues as they arrived in September by air, road, rail and bicycle or the sunny walk from Hope station, for this year's annual Ministers' conference.

In the corner during our conference days there stands a second hand book table, always yielding gems. Among this year's offering was an irresistible collection of old issues of the *Inquirer*. A surprising article from 1936 contained a report regarding women ministers. It began with a lament from across the Atlantic, from Rev. Dr Charles Joy, a major figure among American Unitarians. He was later instrumental in the promotion of the flaming chalice symbol. Here, as an officer of the then American Unitarian Association, he wrote of finding "the prejudice against women ministers so strong that they had been forced to discourage young women from considering the ministry as a career." He went on to appeal to the churches to overcome this "unreasoning prejudice". The *Inquirer* compared this with the situation in 1930s British congregations, just a few years after the formation of the General Assembly. Could we claim to be treating women any better? Seemingly not. In the summer of 1935, the Principal of Unitarian College, Manchester, Rev. Dr Herbert McLachlan had "felt constrained to speak plainly on this matter. The question is – and we are waiting for an answer – do our churches want women in the ministry? Unless there is a marked change in attitude on the part of the churches the day can not be far distant when the college will be driven to consider whether it is justified in expending its resources on the education of women and encouraging them to devote some of their most precious years to conscientious and arduous preparation as students for the ministry." It would presumably have warmed the hearts of both Dr Joy and Dr McLachlan to attend this Ministers' conference eighty years later. Including serving ministers, retired ministers, students for the ministry, and a couple of lay pastors, for the third year in succession there was a majority of women present.

*

I am pleased to learn of a society that I hadn't known existed: The National Federation of Cemetery Friends. This is perhaps not quite what it seems. In many parts of the country there are disused cemeteries, stricken with neglect and vandalism. 'Friends' groups volunteer to take care of such places, for their historical and environmental interest and value, and a national federation keeps them all in supportive touch. I enjoyed a recent visit to the Lister Lane Cemetery in Halifax which, I had been told, had some famous Unitarians buried in it. Our guide was cheery and helpful. "Can you tell me the difference between a burial ground, a graveyard and a cemetery?" I asked. He explained that 'burial ground' is a very broad term but a cemetery (from a Greek word meaning 'sleeping place') is different from a graveyard which means the land beside a parish church. Cemeteries are usually either privately owned or provided by a local authority.

Lister Lane cemetery was intended for nonconformists. There are few crosses on the memorials but many of those splendid Old Testament names that nonconformists favoured: Isaac and Hannah, as well as Uriah, Enoch, Leah and Gad. There were distinct signs of past neglect as the place, which dates from the 1840s had closed in 1960, by which time some 20,000 burials had taken place. The Friends have worked hard since 2000 and the much improved land and graves now have Grade 2 listed status., and have been named as 'significant' by the Association of Significant Cemeteries in Europe.

*

Among Unitarians buried there is Rev. Francis England Millson (1829-1910). He served the now closed Northgate End Unitarian Chapel, Halifax and published its 200th anniversary history in 1896. Our guide told us, "He was very broadminded, he once gave a sermon to raise funds for Charles Bradlaugh, the renowned atheist, when the latter was very ill." Bradlaugh (1833-1891) travelled the country lecturing on atheism and was eventually elected an MP, several times. It was some years, however, before he could take his parliamentary seat as he refused to swear the oath of allegiance. So, it is by no means a modern feature of Unitarian ministers to be sympathetic towards atheists. Millson's fundraising sermon raised £10.

*

At long last the work to remove graves from the road beside Cross Street Chapel, Manchester seems to have been completed. The scaffolding and screening which have shrouded the building for many months are now gone and the congregation can be seen to be alive and well, with twice-weekly worship, regular music recitals and other activities.

*

Pondering our latter days and end sometimes evokes humour. The *Inquirer* of April 1936 has the story of an astronomer who was lecturing in a small Scottish town on the wonders of the heavens. He showed awe-inspiring lantern slides and recited brain-reeling facts, distances, dimensions. More than once he emphasised, in somewhat sepulchral tones, that in 700,000,000 years, the world would be dead.

At the close of the lecture, a farmer stood up looking very worried. This reiterated prediction of the impending doom of the earth seemed to have made him anxious. To the lecturer he said:

"Hoo many years did ye say it would be before the world was cauld and deid?"

"Seven hundred million years," said the lecturer, in still more sepulchral tones.

The farmer sat down suddenly with a sigh of relief. "Thank God," he said, mopping his brow with a handkerchief, "I thought ye said *seven million*."

October 2015

Epilogue

This collection of diary or notebook pieces has been produced at a time when the world of printing and publications is in a period of serious transition. All the main newspapers of the UK have reported a decline in sales in recent years, and give a range of reasons for it. In no cases that I have read do any of the observers of the media world blame this decline on the content of the papers. It is the rise and rise of TV news and current affairs programmes that is seen as significant, plus the arrival of online publications and social media. These are regarded as the main factors challenging the producers of newspapers, magazines and journals, both for the content that they produce and the means by which they distribute it.

Few if any commentators on this situation regard this as a doom-laden crisis period. No-one is forecasting the end of hard copy. The main view taken is that electronic publications and print media will continue, side by side, to serve their readers for the foreseeable future.

For my own part, I confess to being somewhat conservative. I am a computer user, I use emails a lot and I dip in and out of the social media somewhat sporadically. But it is the arrival of my favourite newspapers through the letterbox each morning, and the fortnightly sight of the familiar envelope containing *The Inquirer*, that remain the most satisfying. Even so, I realise that newspapers have a short life-span. Someone once pointed out to me that the Greek word for newspapers has the same root as our word 'ephemera'. Then again, it is a common experience to pick up an out of date paper and find oneself quickly engrossed by its contents.

As one who enjoys writing, and, almost as an act of defiance, I retain an affection for the famous statement by Beatrice Warde. I first saw this up on the wall of an old-fashioned print shop, with its clanking, black machinery and the smell of ink and warm paper. I came across it again some years later in the enthralling book on fonts, *Just My Type* by Simon Garfield:

THIS IS
A PRINTING OFFICE
CROSSROADS OF CIVILISATION
REFUGE OF ALL THE ARTS
AGAINST THE RAVAGES OF TIME
ARMOURY OF FEARLESS TRUTH
AGAINST WHISPERING RUMOUR
INCESSANT TRUMPET OF TRADE
FROM THIS PLACE WORDS MAY FLY ABROAD
NOT TO PERISH ON WAVES OF SOUND
NOT TO VARY WITH THE WRITER'S HAND
BUT FIXED IN TIME HAVING BEEN VERIFIED IN PROOF
FRIEND YOU STAND ON SACRED GROUND
THIS IS A PRINTING OFFICE

Beatrice Warde (1900-1969)

In certain moods I can detect an almost laughable high-mindedness in this strongly worded statement and I understand that it has often been parodied. But in more serious moments I acknowledge the totally transforming effect on human history of the arrival of the printing press, and all that it implied. It is utterly impossible to imagine the world without printed words. So, once again I find myself viewing something as both amusing and serious, simultaneously.

What I am getting round to saying, I suppose, is, if you have done, thank you for reading this book. For more reasons than I can possibly convey, I remain convinced that ours is, without doubt, a funny old world.